THE DUTY OF FAIR REPRE- SENTATION

Papers from the National
Conference on the Duty of
Fair Representation,
sponsored by the New York
State School of Industrial and
Labor Relations, Cornell
University

Automation House
New York City
April 28 and 29, 1977

Jean T. McKelvey, editor

New York State School
of Industrial
& Labor Relations
Cornell University
1977

First printing, 1977
Second printing, 1978

Price: $6.95 paperbound, $10.95 hardbound

Copies of this publication may be ordered from
ILR Publications Division
New York State School of Industrial and Labor Relations
Cornell University, Box 1000
Ithaca, New York 14853

Cover design by Michael Rider

Contents

v   Preface

1   Introduction
    Jean T. McKelvey

8   The Duty of Fair Representation:
    An Overview
    Benjamin Aaron

25   The Origins of the Concept of
     the Duty of Fair Representation
     James E. Jones, Jr.

44   The Conflict between the
     Duty of Fair Representation and
     the Limitations on Union
     Self-Government
     Judith P. Vladeck

55   The Implications of Hines v.
     Anchor Motor Freight
     Richard Lipsitz

60   The Individual Employee's
     Rights under the Collective
     Agreement: What Constitutes
     Fair Representation?
     Clyde W. Summers

84   The Duty of Fair Representation
     in Arbitration
     Robert J. Rabin

97   Enforcement of the
     Right to Fair Representation:
     Alternative Forums
     David Y. Klein

105   The Absence of Fair Representation
      Thomas R. Donahue

112   Contributors

Preface

The intervention of the courts in internal union and union-management relations is a question of growing concern to practitioners in industrial and labor relations. Encouraged by legislative and administrative rulings designed to protect individual rights, workers increasingly bring lawsuits against their unions and employers outside the normal channels of dispute settlement. "The duty of fair representation" doctrine under which courts review grievance and organizational decisions was the theme of a conference sponsored by the New York State School of Industrial and Labor Relations, Cornell University, at Automation House in New York City in April 1977. Featuring presentations by leading scholars, neutrals, and advocates, the conference was designed to explore the legal implications and the organizational impact of court decisions and governmental policy.

Professor Jean McKelvey, a founder of the ILR School and past president of the National Academy of Arbitrators, planned and chaired the conference.

Cornell's ILR School was established by the New York State Legislature in 1945 with a mandate to provide resident instruction, research, and adult education to advance understanding of industrial and labor relations. In keeping with this mission, the School conducts courses, conferences, and workshops for practitioners focusing on key issues in the field. Publication of the proceedings of this conference aims to reach labor union officials, managers, attorneys, and academicians who are concerned with the important question of the duty of fair representation.

Lois S. Gray
Associate Dean and Director of
Extension and Public Service
New York State School of Industrial
and Labor Relations
Cornell University

Introduction

Jean T. McKelvey

On April 28 and 29, 1977, the New York State School of Industrial and
Labor Relations sponsored a national conference on The Duty of Fair
Representation for international union officers and staff and for union
attorneys, which was held at Automation House in New York City. In
order to encourage full discussion, attendance at the conference was
limited by invitation.

The theme of this conference was suggested, in part, by the
Wingspread Conference on the Future of Labor Arbitration sponsored
by the American Arbitration Association (AAA) and held in November
1975. In summarizing one of the papers at the Wingspread Conference,
Gerald Aksen, General Counsel of the AAA, noted: "Always a recurring
theme in labor publications, arbitration and individual rights cannot be
overexplored."[1] Those who planned the Cornell conference decided to
explore further the dimensions of the duty of fair representation. They
were fortunate in enlisting as speakers four preeminent legal scholars and
prominent union attorneys whose practice as advocates involved the
defense of their union clients against charges brought by individuals that
their union had breached its duty to represent them fairly in the processing of their grievances or according them due process in presenting their
grievances in an arbitration proceeding.

This volume contains the papers delivered at the Cornell conference.
What is remarkable about them, in my opinion, is the high degree of
integration which emerges from reading them in sequence and reflecting
on them as a whole and their concentration on the dimensions of the duty
of fair representation as well as the divergence of points of view on the
significance of its impact on traditional concepts and practices of collective
bargaining and contract administration.

In his comprehensive overview of the subject, Benjamin Aaron first
reviews the evolution and the present state of the law on the duty of fair
representation in both the private and public sectors. He then goes on to
deal with some unresolved questions. He notes that one of the most
pressing questions relates to a clarification of "exactly what types of
conduct constitute a violation of the duty," observing that "on this point
the Supreme Court has spoken with such impenetrable ambiguity" that
the lower federal courts "are understandably in disagreement as to what

---

1. *The Future of Labor Arbitration in America* (New York: American Arbitration Association, 1976), p. xiv.

1

the law is." The confusion generated by the Supreme Court concerns such questions as whether there must be a showing of bad faith before an action for breach of the duty can be brought, whether mere negligence constitutes a breach, and whether negligence should be distinguished from the exercise of poor judgment. Aaron's answers to these and other questions will be of interest to scholars and practitioners alike.

A scholarly analysis of the origins of the concept of the duty of fair representation by James E. Jones, Jr., notes that the doctrine emerged from early National Mediation Board (NMB), National Labor Relations Board (NLRB), and Supreme Court decisions concerning invidious racial discrimination practiced by unions or reflected in collective bargaining agreements. The sources of this duty, he observes, lie neither in the Constitution nor in statute, but spring from common law concepts of agency and trust.

Now that racial discrimination has been proscribed by statute, the concept has been expanded to encompass other forms of what Jones labels arbitrary or irrational discrimination practiced against individual union members in grievance handling and arbitration proceedings. Like Aaron he notes the "slippery dimensions" of the duty of fair representation, particularly the question of using negligence as a standard for measuring the duty.

Following these analyses of the law, two union attorneys present their points of view on the impact of the judicial decisions on the structure and functioning of unions. Judith P. Vladeck's primary concern as an advocate is that by imposing higher and higher standards of fair representation, the courts have displayed their failure to understand and take into account the nature of unions as institutions, especially the fact that they are governed by laymen and workers from the shop who are untutored in the niceties and fine points of the law. In Vladeck's view the courts do not recognize that union stewards and business agents are chosen because of popularity, not literacy in writing grievances, and that once an individual's grievance proceeds beyond the beginning stages, it may be too late for the union to avoid subsequent charges of perfunctory or negligent handling. Vladeck illustrates her concern over the "woeful ignorance" of courts, administrative agencies, and Congress concerning the collective rights of unions by citing such areas of intervention as limiting the right of unions to discharge members who engage in strike-breaking; interfering with the union's right to discipline members who encourage dual unionism; interfering with grants of special privilege such as super-seniority to shop stewards; modifying a union's own requirements for eligibility for candidacy for union office; and permitting employer financing of individual employee suits against unions.

According to Vladeck this basic lack of judicial understanding of the nature and purpose of labor organizations coupled with the imposition of increasing standards of union accountability in handling grievances has created an irreconcilable conflict between the duty of fair representation and the limitations of union self-government.

A different point of view from Vladeck's is expressed by Richard Lipsitz, also an advocate, who compares standards of the duty of fair representation before and after the famous *Hines* v. *Anchor Motor Freight, Inc.* case. Noting the pre-*Hines* standard that if a union acted in good faith, although mistakenly, in processing an individual's grievance up to or including arbitration, it had discharged its duty of fair representation and hence a cause of action against a union or an employer would fail, Lipsitz interprets *Hines* as creating a substantial and radical alteration of the standards in *Vaca* v. *Sipes* by expanding them to include the union's lack of diligence in investigating facts and marshalling arguments in presenting cases in arbitration.

Unlike Vladeck who deplores this development, Lipsitz supports the imposition of strict standards of representation upon unions, holding that in the long run more rigorous standards will strengthen union democracy. Also in contrast to Vladeck, who favors a weakening of judicial intervention, Lipsitz calls for a reform of union practices and policies by suggesting such innovations as the employment of an ombudsman to evaluate the merits of an employee's grievance, training union representatives in investigating grievances at the pre-arbitration stage and presenting the facts effectively in arbitration, and creating more public review boards as an alternative to litigation. Thus the debate is squarely joined on the issue of whether it is the law or the quality of union representation that should be changed to accommodate the conflict between the duty of fair representation and the institution of collective bargaining.

This conflict is addressed in greater detail by Clyde W. Summers, who analyzes the question of what constitutes fair representation in the processing of grievances, and Robert J. Rabin, who discusses the duty of fair representation in arbitration proceedings.

Summers's solution to the conflict is based on his distinguishing between the negotiation of a contract, where because of statutory policy and court and board decisions the union must be afforded a broad range of discretion in resolving conflicts of interest within its ranks, and the administration of the contract, where the union must be held to stricter standards of accountability to its members because by contract, rather than by statute, the union has acquired exclusive control of the grievance procedure, thereby depriving an individual of his ability to enforce his contractual rights and obligating the union to act for, not against, his interests.

To illustrate his position favoring resort to the tightest possible standards for measuring the quality of the union's duty of fair representation, Summers uses seven sample or hypothetical cases. While not exhaustive, they provide a focus for applying the general standards enunciated by the Supreme Court to particular fact situations. From these cases, according to Summers, the following six standards or principles seem clearly to emerge:

1. The individual must receive all rights and benefits guaranteed him under the clear language of the contract. These rights cannot be waived by informal agreements to ignore or change them.

2. Although the union has the right to settle a grievance involving ambiguous contract language, it has an obligation to apply such a settlement consistently, since "settlement of similar grievances on different terms is discriminatory and violates the union's duty to represent all employees equally."

3. The union has no duty to process every grievance to arbitration when it has made a good-faith judgment that the grievance is frivolous, trivial or wholly without merit. But the individual has a right to equal access to the grievance procedure including the right to arbitration for similar grievances of equal merit.

4. Settlement of grievances for improper motives such as personal hostility, political opposition or racial prejudice constitutes bad faith in and of itself regardless of the merits of the grievance.

5. An individual union member has a right to have his grievance settled on its merits. Hence a union that trades an individual's meritorious grievance in exchange for settlement of another individual's or group's grievance violates the union's duty of fair representation.

6. Although a union can make a good-faith judgment that an individual's grievance lacks merit, it nevertheless has an obligation to use reasonable care and diligence in investigating the grievance before it decides that it is nonmeritorious.

In Summers's view these standards provide more workable and refined guidelines for measuring the dimensions of the duty of fair representation in concrete situations than do the vaguer principles and standards enunciated by the Supreme Court. Moreover, they protect the individual's right to fair representation in the handling of his grievance as well as permitting the union sufficient flexibility to discharge its responsibilities in administering the collective bargaining agreement.

Rabin's paper deals with the impact of the duty of fair representation on the conduct of arbitration hearings. He is especially concerned about the growing trend toward judicial scrutiny of the arbitration process as revealed not by the big name cases decided by the Supreme Court, which he finds to be extreme and unique examples of perfunctory grievance handling, but by the decisions of the lower courts and the NLRB. His empirical study of these less well known and more routine cases leads him to conclude that the volume of litigation over the duty of fair representation is "alarming," having reached a rate of seventy such reported cases a year, almost a third of which involve challenges to the way in which grievances are handled in the arbitration forum. Asking the question how lax a union's performance in arbitration must be before it falls under the rubric of "perfunctory or arbitrary" treatment, he answers that the union must use "rational" standards to determine that a grievance should not be arbitrated and that judicial scrutiny of arbitration proceedings should be limited to cases involving evidence of hostility towards the grievant or inexcusable omissions of fact and argument which jeopardize the individual's chance of success in having his grievance decided on its merits. To stem the tide of increasing judicial intervention in the arbitration process, Rabin makes the following suggestions:

1. The arbitrator has a responsibility to assure that the individual has been fairly represented in the hearing. This means that the arbitrator who suspects that the union is weak in its advocacy must take the initiative in asking questions, requesting more evidence, and even calling for witnesses whose testimony may be crucial to the case.

2. Where the union is faced with a conflict of interest between individuals or groups, the individual grievant should be allowed to intervene in the hearing with his own counsel.

3. If this kind of tripartite proceeding is not feasible, at the least the individual and his counsel should be permitted to discuss various approaches and evidence with the union before the hearing.

4. When the arbitrator anticipates potential problems of fair representation in a particular case, he or she should require a transcript of the proceedings.

5. Unions should incorporate an independent body within their internal appeals system such as a public review board or an ombudsman who by assuring individuals an objective review of their grievances might reduce their recourse to litigation.

Picking up this theme of the desirability of creating public review boards as alternative forums to the courts, David Y. Klein, Counsel to the Public Review Board (PRB) of the United Auto Workers (UAW), stated as his hypothesis that public review boards as constituted today do not qualify as alternative forums at least in the area of the duty of fair representation, but might with some modifications of their jurisdiction be accepted by the courts and the NLRB as an alternative forum to which they might defer. Noting that 33 to 40 percent of the appeals to the UAW board involve the processing of grievances, Klein pointed out that the board's jurisdiction over these appeals is limited by the UAW Constitution to cases involving fraud, discrimination or collusion with management—a bad-faith standard which is much narrower than today's judicial standards of arbitrary, perfunctory or negligent handling of grievances. In fact, in the last twenty years only one appellant has prevailed before the board in a claimed breach of the duty of fair representation, in that case the refusal of the union to submit his grievance to arbitration.

Since the PRB's standards no longer track those of the courts, Klein argues that in many, if not most, of these cases resort to the PRB will be futile. Hence he predicts that there will be even fewer cases in which the courts will require individuals to exhaust their internal procedures before bringing suits against the union for breach of the duty and against the employer for breach of contract.

To remedy this problem Klein suggests that the UAW could amend its Constitution to provide that members' claims of breach of the duty of fair representation could be processed within the internal union justice system up to and including the PRB. This would make the board an alternative forum to which the courts might defer.

Klein notes further that although the board lacks jurisdiction over the employer, so far as the scope of its remedial power is concerned, this weakness has been redressed by the last round of contract negotiations between the UAW and each of the "big three" auto companies. These agreements now provide that the companies will reinstate a grievance into the grievance procedure when an internal union tribunal has found that the union has breached its duty of fair representation in processing the grievance. Such a solution is not only ingenious but also of mutual benefit to both parties since a union which is found to be in breach of its duty of fair representation also implicates the employer who may then be sued for breach of contract.

A vigorous plea for changes in our labor policy and labor laws to afford greater representation rights to unorganized workers is voiced by Thomas Donahue in his paper, which was the luncheon speech at the conference.

As these brief summaries indicate, the authors of these papers have made a notable contribution to the exploration of the dimensions of the duty of fair representation. Despite their differences, they exhibit remarkable agreement on the need for improving the quality of union representation and for establishing impartial review boards to function within the internal union justice system. Whether their calls for reform will be heeded is a matter that should concern unions and employers alike.

The sponsors of the Cornell conference are grateful to the authors for their superb analyses of the problems emerging from the duty of fair representation and for their recommendations and proposals for dealing with the discharge of this duty. Finally, special thanks are due to Rochelle Semel of the metropolitan office for her handling of the entire administration of the conference.

The Duty of Fair Representation: An Overview

Benjamin Aaron

The duty of fair representation is imposed on the exclusive bargaining representative of the bargaining unit; but the members of that unit and the employer are also affected in fundamental ways by its application. In addition, the doctrine of the duty of fair representation has ramifications in other areas: the nature of the duty and its scope; the jurisdiction of courts, administrative agencies, and arbitrators over cases involving the duty; the various types of remedies for breach of the duty; and the respective liabilities of unions and employers, once breach of the duty has been established. More important still, the doctrine embraces the issue of the legal nature of a collective bargaining agreement and the rights and obligations of employers, unions, and employees arising thereunder.

This overview will not attempt to cover the entire range of problems associated with the duty of fair representation. Instead it will present a brief, somewhat oversimplified, summary of the present law on the duty of fair representation and will then focus on the developments and attendant problems associated with that duty that are of particular interest.

Fair Representation in a Nutshell

The duty of fair representation is a judicial invention. It is not specifically mentioned in either the Railway Labor Act (RLA) or the National Labor Relations Act (NLRA); yet it derives from Section 2 of the RLA[1] and Section 9(a) of the NLRA.[2] The Supreme Court has held — in order to

---

1. 48 Stat. 1185, 45 U.S.C. § 152, Fourth, provides in part: "The majority of any craft or class of employees shall have the right to determine who shall be the representative of the craft or class for the purposes of this Chapter." Minority groups within the union, or nonunion groups within the bargaining unit, are not allowed to choose another representative or to engage in individual bargaining over matters properly within the scope of collective bargaining. Order of R.R. Telegraphers v. Railway Express Agency, 321 U.S. 342 (1944).

2. 29 U.S.C. § 159(a) (1970 and Supp. IV 1974) provides in part: "Representatives designated or selected for the purposes of collective bargaining by the majority of employees

avoid questions of the constitutionality of statutory delegation of the power of exclusive collective bargaining representation to unions — that such power must be exercised in the interest and on behalf of all those represented by the union "without hostile discrimination, fairly, impartially, and in good faith."[3]

The exclusive statutory representative is not barred from making agreements that may have unfavorable effects on some members of the bargaining unit, all of whom cannot have identical interests or equal qualifications. Differences within the group are bound to arise, and the complete satisfaction of all who are represented is quite unlikely. Therefore, the Court has stipulated the statutory representative must be allowed a "wide range of reasonableness" in the exercise of its judgment on behalf of the unit it represents, "subject always to complete good faith and honesty of purpose."[4]

The first Supreme Court decision to explicate the duty of fair representation was *Steele* v. *Louisville & Nashville Railroad*,[5] a case arising under the RLA. Most of the early cases involved unions covered by that statute. In one of those, *Elgin, Joliet & Eastern Railway* v. *Burley*,[6] without being specifically authorized to do so, the union had compromised a number of money claims filed by employees they represented. A divided Court held that the union could not lawfully settle claims based on existing rights without being authorized in "some legally sufficient way" to act in the claimants' behalf.[7] In short, the union's exclusive authority to make or change collective bargaining agreements did not extend to "changing them with retroactive effects upon accrued rights or claims."[8] Most subsequent decisions have failed to emphasize this distinction, however.[9]

In succeeding decisions under the RLA the Supreme Court held, first, that a union owes even to persons outside the bargaining unit it represents, who may or may not be represented by another labor organi-

---

in a unit appropriate for such purposes, shall be the exclusive representatives of all employees in such unit for the purposes of collective bargaining in respect to rates of pay, wages, hours of employment, or other conditions of employment." Minority groups within the union, or nonunion employees within the bargaining unit, stand on the same footing as their counterparts covered by the RLA, *supra* footnote 1. Medo Photo Supply Corp. v. NLRB, 321 U.S. 678 (1944); J. I. Case v. NLRB, 321 U.S. 332 (1944).

3. Steele v. Louisville & Nashville R.R., 323 U.S. 192 (1944) at 204.
4. Ford Motor Co. v. Huffman, 345 U.S. 330 (1953) at 338.
5. 323 U.S. 192 (1944).
6. 325 U.S. 711 (1945), *aff'd on rehearing*, 327 U.S. 661 (1946).
7. Id. at 738.
8. Id. at 739.
9. See, for example, Price v. International Bhd. of Teamsters, 457 F.2d 605 (3d Cir. 1972) at 610, wherein the court said: "A court will defer to arbitrators or committees when they are exercising their delegated power to decide unforeseen or unresolved problems arising out of gaps or content in the contract. However, it will not allow them to ignore provisions embodied in the agreement: the basic contract rights must be enforced."

zation, an affirmative duty not to use its power to cause an employer to discriminate against them solely on racial grounds,[10] and, second, that the duty of fair representation applies not only to the negotiation of new contract terms but also to the application of terms of existing agreements.[11] The Court also made explicit what it had only implied earlier: that the Norris–LaGuardia Act did not deprive federal courts of jurisdiction "to enforce by injunction [minority] petitioners' rights to nondiscriminatory representation by their statutory representative."[12]

In 1956 the Supreme Court held that the same duty of fair representation imposed by the RLA was required by the NLRA.[13] The National Labor Relations Board (NLRB) did not decide that a violation of this duty constituted an unfair labor practice, however, until 1962, when it held in a divided vote in *Miranda Fuel Co.*,[14] that Section 7 of the NLRA gives employees the right to be free from unfair, irrelevant, or invidious treatment by their exclusive bargaining representative in matters affecting their employment; that Section 8(b)(1)(a) accordingly prohibits exclusive bargaining representatives from taking such proscribed action against any employee; and that a statutory bargaining agent violates Section 8(b)(2) when, for any of the proscribed reasons, it attempts to cause or does cause an employer to derogate the employment status of an employee. The Board also held that any employer yielding to a union's request to discriminate against an employee for any of the proscribed reasons violates Sections 8(a)(1) and (3). In subsequent cases involving a union's refusal to process grievances solely because the grievants were Negroes, the Board found an additional violation of Section 8(b)(3).[15]

Discussing if the Board was right or wrong in its conclusion that violation of the duty of fair representation constitutes one or more unfair labor practices is beyond the manageable scope of this paper.[16] It must thus suffice to note that despite being rebuffed by the second circuit,[17] the Board's assertions have been upheld by the fifth, seventh, and D.C.

10. Brotherhood of R.R. Trainmen v. Howard, 343 U.S. 768 (1952) at 774.
11. Conley v. Gibson, 355 U.S. 41 (1957) at 46.
12. Graham v. Brotherhood of Locomotive Firemen, 338 U.S. 232 (1949).
13. Syres v. Oil Workers Int'l Union, 223 F.2d 739 (5th Cir. 1955), *rev'd and remanded per curiam,* 350 U.S. 892 (1956).
14. 140 NLRB 181 (1962), *enforcement denied,* 326 F.2d 172 (2d Cir. 1963).
15. NLRB v. Local 1367, Int'l Longshoremen's Ass'n, 368 F.2d 1010 (5th Cir. 1966), *cert. denied,* 389 U.S. 837 (1967); Local 12, United Rubber Workers v. NLRB, 368 F.2d 12 (5th Cir. 1966), *cert. denied,* 389 U.S. 837 (1967).
16. For differing views, see Michael I. Sovern, "Race Discrimination and the National Labor Relations Act: The Brave New World of Miranda," in *New York University Sixteenth Annual Conference on Labor* (1963), p. 3, and Note, "Administrative Enforcement of the Right to Fair Representation: The Miranda Case," *University of Pennsylvania Law Review* 112 (1964):711.
17. NLRB v. Miranda Fuel Co., 326 F.2d 172 (2d Cir. 1963).

circuits[18] (although not always on the same grounds relied upon by the Board) and seem now to be recognized at least tacitly by the Supreme Court.[19]

The NLRA purports to give the NLRB exclusive jurisdiction over unfair labor practices, and, although riddled with exceptions, the preemption rule originally enunciated by the Supreme Court in *San Diego Building Trades Council v. Garmon*[20] has not been repudiated. It states that "when an activity is arguably subject to §7 or §8 of the Act, the States as well as the federal courts must defer to the exclusive competence of the... Board...."[21]

One major exception to this rule was carved out by the Court when it held in *Smith v. Evening News*[22] that a suit could be brought for breach of a collective bargaining agreement under Section 301 of the Labor Management Relations Act (LMRA) — which concerns suits for violation of contracts between employers and labor organizations — even though the alleged violation would also constitute an arguable or conceded unfair labor practice.

In another case a group of employees adversely affected by an agreement on the merger of two seniority lists made in an amalgamation of two companies by a union-employer grievance committee brought an action under Section 301.[23] They charged, first, that the union-employer grievance committee had violated the collective bargaining agreement and, second, that the committee's decision was brought about by dishonest union conduct in violation of its duty of fair representation. Although ruling unanimously against the plaintiffs on the merits, the Supreme Court held, first, that an action based on a claim that a union has violated its duty of fair representation may be maintained under Section 301 and, second, that, as stated in *Evening News*, even if the alleged breach of contract also constitutes an unfair labor practice, the courts are not ousted of their Section 301 jurisdiction to try the case.

The next major statement by the Supreme Court on the subject of the duty of fair representation was made in *Vaca v. Sipes*.[24] In that case the plaintiff, Benjamin Owens, had been hospitalized for hypertension and heart disease. He was eventually discharged from the hospital and given a statement by his physician that he could return to work, but the employer

---

18. See cases cited in footnote 15 *supra*.
19. In Vaca v. Sipes, 386 U.S. 171 (1967), the Court assumed, without deciding, that the union's alleged breach of its duty of fair representation in that case, if proved, would have constituted an unfair labor practice.
20. 359 U.S. 236 (1959).
21. Id. at 245.
22. 371 U.S. 195 (1962).
23. Humphrey v. Moore, 375 U.S. 335 (1964).
24. 386 U.S. 171 (1967).

refused to take him back on the ground that its doctor considered it unsafe for Owens to perform his job, which was physically demanding. Owens filed a grievance, which his union processed through every step up to arbitration. At that stage the employer advised that it would take Owens back only if a thorough physical examination showed that he was able to perform his job. Accordingly, the union paid for such an examination by a specialist chosen by Owens. The specialist reported that Owens's blood pressure was so high that any work would be hazardous to his health, and the union then decided not to take the case to arbitration.

Owens filed suit in a Missouri court against the union for refusing to take his grievance to arbitration; he asked for both compensation for lost wages and punitive damages. At the trial he introduced evidence of his capability to do strenuous work. The union relied solely on the defense of its good faith in deciding not to arbitrate the grievance. The jury decided in Owens's favor for the full amount claimed, but the trial court set aside the verdict on the ground that Owens's claim was within the exclusive jurisdiction of the NLRB. After the trial, Owens vindicated the judgment of the neutral specialist by dying of a "cardiovascular accident due to hypertension." His administrator, Sipes, appealed from the trial court's decision to the Supreme Court of Missouri, which reinstated the verdict on the ground that the union's refusal to arbitrate Owens's grievance was an unfair labor practice, and that the evidence was sufficient to support the jury's verdict that he had been healthy enough to work. The United States Supreme Court later reversed the decision and held that the union had not breached its duty of fair representation.

In writing the Supreme Court's majority opinion Justice White covered a number of important issues. He declared that the NLRB did not have exclusive jurisdiction of the controversy, noting that the preemption doctrine "has never been rigidly applied to cases where it could not fairly be inferred that Congress intended exclusive jurisdiction to lie" with that agency, as in actions for breach of contract under Section 301.[25] Asserting that the decision to preempt federal and state court jurisdiction over a given class of cases "must depend upon the nature of the particular interests being asserted and the effect upon the administration of national labor policies and concurrent judicial and administrative remedies," Justice White concluded that the preemption doctrine was not applicable to cases involving the alleged violation of the union's duty of fair representation.[26]

The reasons underlying the Court's conclusion are persuasive. Justice White pointed out, first, that the doctrine of duty of fair representa-

25. Id. at 179.
26. Id. at 180.

tion was conceived and developed by the federal courts, and that suits alleging breach of the duty remained judicially cognizable even after the NLRB acquired jurisdiction over union unfair labor practices; second, that when the NLRB finally decided that union violations of the duty were unfair labor practices, it applied the doctrine as developed by the courts; third, that the Board's expertise in this area was not substantially greater than that of the courts; fourth, that preemption would create the possibility that an employee injured by arbitrary or discriminatory union conduct might not receive an impartial review of his claim because of the unreviewable discretion of the Board's general counsel not to issue an unfair labor practice complaint if he thought the injury specified was "insubstantial";[27] and, fifth, that in many instances whether a union has violated its duty of fair representation will be a critical issue in a Section 301 action against an employer for breach of contract — an action over which the courts have jurisdiction even though the breach of contract may also constitute an unfair labor practice.

Another issue raised by *Vaca* was whether federal or state law should define the nature of the union's duty of fair representation and the remedy for its breach. The Court held that federal law is to apply. Relying on its previous decisions in *Humphrey* v. *Moore* and *Ford Motor Co.* v. *Huffman,* as well as on the writings of scholars analyzing the union's role in the negotiation and administration of collective bargaining agreements, Justice White stated that a breach of the statutory duty of fair representation occurs only when a union's conduct toward a member of the bargaining unit is "arbitrary, discriminatory, or in bad faith."[28] He could see no "substantial danger to the interests of the individual employee if his statutory agent is given the contractual power honestly and in good faith to settle grievances short of arbitration."[29]

In reaching this decision the Court considered — and expressly rejected — the theory that every employee should have the right to have his grievance taken to arbitration. Justice White explained that adoption of this principle would substantially undermine the collective bargaining relationship between union and employer, for it would destroy the employer's confidence in the union's authority, return the individual grievant "to the vagaries of independent and unsystematic negotiation," and very likely overburden the arbitration process to the point of rendering it inoperable.[30]

Justice White conceded that an order compelling the union and the

---

27. See Administrative Decision of General Counsel, Case No. K-610, 1956–57 CCH NLRB para. 54,059 (Aug. 13, 1956).
28. 386 U.S. 171 at 190.
29. Id. at 192.
30. Id. at 191.

employer to arbitrate the employee's grievance is one remedy available when the union's breach of its duty of fair representation has been proved; but he saw no reason inflexibly to require arbitration in all such cases. He explained:

In some cases...at least part of the employees' damages may be attributable to the union's breach of duty, and an arbitrator may have no power under the bargaining agreement to award such damages against the union. In other cases, the arbitrable issues may be substantially resolved in the course of trying the fair representation controversy. In such situations, the court should be free to decide the contractual claim and to award the employee appropriate damages or equitable relief.[31]

A major portion of the *Vaca* opinion was devoted to a detailed consideration of the problems of an individual employee who complains of unfair treatment by his employer, his union, or both. Justice White reiterated the principle, announced two years earlier in *Republic Steel Corp.* v. *Maddox*,[32] that an employee must at least attempt to exhaust contractual grievance and arbitration procedures before bringing an action under Section 301. He recognized, however, that "because these contractual remedies have been devised and are often controlled by the union and the employer, they may well prove unsatisfactory or unworkable for the individual grievant."[33] He noted, therefore, that a discharged employee is relieved of the exhaustion requirement if the employer's conduct "amounts to a repudiation of those contractual procedures";[34] or if, as was true in *Vaca*, "the union has sole power under the contract to invoke the higher stages of the grievance procedure, *and* if . . . the employee-plaintiff has been prevented from exhausting his contractual remedies by the union's *wrongful* refusal to process the grievance."[35]

Although the employer in *Vaca* had done nothing to prevent Owens's exhaustion of his contractual remedies, it had allegedly violated the agreement by discharging him without just cause, Justice White explained. He concluded that Congress had never intended either "to confer upon unions...unlimited discretion to deprive injured employees of all remedies for breach of contract" or "to shield employers from the natural consequences of their breaches of bargaining agreements by wrongful union conduct in the enforcement of such agreements."[36]

It follows from this conclusion that a wrongfully discharged employee may sue his employer without exhausting his contract remedies, provided he can prove that the union violated its duty to represent him fairly in the handling of his grievance. This is true even if it is assumed, as

---

31. Id. at 196.
32. 379 U.S. 650 (1965).
33. 386 U.S. 171 at 185.
34. Id.
35. Id.
36. Id. at 186.

it was by a majority of the Court in *Vaca*, that the union's breach of its duty was also an unfair labor practice, because the employee's suit against the employer remains a Section 301 suit within the jurisdiction of the courts.

The problem of determining appropriate damages in such a suit was another reason mentioned in Justice White's opinion for not applying the preemption doctrine. He reasoned that in situations in which the union's failure to represent fairly has enhanced or contributed to the employee's injury, there would be no sense in preventing a court from awarding damages against both the union and the employer. If the NLRB had exclusive jurisdiction, it would be "compelled in many cases either to remedy injuries arising out of a breach of contract, a task which Congress has not assigned to it, or to leave the individual employee without remedy for the union's wrong."[37]

Finally, although the Court held that the union had not violated its duty of fair representation, and therefore that neither it nor the employer was liable for damages, Justice White went on to consider what damages would have been appropriate if the union had in fact breached its duty. He found that the jury's verdict of punitive damages against the union could not have been sustained in any case, because it assessed against the union damages attributable solely to the employer's alleged breach of contract. The correct approach, he declared, would be to charge the union only for increases in the damages chargeable to the employer caused by the union's wrongful conduct.

The most recent occasion for the Supreme Court to discuss the duty of fair representation was provided in 1976 in *Hines* v. *Anchor Motor Freight, Inc.*[38] In that case a discharge of several employees for theft was sustained by a bipartite committee consisting of equal numbers of union and employer representatives. The evidence in the subsequent trial of a Section 301 suit brought by the dismissed employees against both the local and international unions and the employer showed that the local had at the very least been negligent in the handling of the grievance; that the dismissed employees were in fact innocent of the offense for which they had been discharged; and that the employer had acted in good faith. The only issue before the Supreme Court was the employer's liability. On that point the sixth circuit concluded that the finality of the bipartite committee's decision must be observed because there was no evidence of any misconduct on the employer's part; the Supreme Court reversed.

Again speaking for a majority of the Court, Justice White held that if both an erroneous discharge and the union's breach of duty "tainting" the decision of the joint committee could be proved, the plaintiffs were

37. Id. at 187–88.
38. 424 U.S. 554 (1976). See Richard Lipsitz's chapter in this book for a thorough discussion of this case.

entitled to an appropriate remedy against the employer as well as the union. Justice Rehnquist and Chief Justice Burger dissented in an opinion written by the former, who declared that in *Hines* "the Court has cast aside the finality of arbitration decisions and established a new policy of encouraging challenges to arbitration decrees by the losing party on the ground that he was not properly represented."[39]

The Duty of Fair Representation in the Public Sector

The application of the duty of fair representation is somewhat different in the public sector. Although the guarantees of the federal Bill of Rights, made binding on the states by the Fourteenth Amendment, of course, do not apply to purely private employment, they are fully enforceable in any situation in which the government — whether federal, state, county, or municipal — is the actual employer or has an interest in the employing enterprise sufficient to constitute what the courts refer to as "state action."[40]

One may hypothesize that when the bargaining representatives in the public sector do achieve the same power over the processing of grievances that is exercised by their private sector counterparts, however, they should be held subject to the same duty of fair representation. This in fact appears to be the case. In *Kaufman* v. *Goldberg*,[41] a social worker in New York, who claimed to have been punitively transferred and demoted, with a loss of seniority, filed a grievance alleging a violation of the applicable collective bargaining agreement. Alleging that the union had refused to take the case to arbitration because he was not a member, the grievant brought suit to vacate the denial of his grievance and to secure reinstatement to his former job. The court found that in fact the grievant had never asked the union to take the case to arbitration; therefore, it dismissed the suit. Nevertheless, in an elaborate dictum in which it quoted extensively from private sector precedents, the court declared that the union, as the employee's "sole and exclusive" bargaining representative, was under a duty "to entertain and consider ... [his grievance] on the merits so as to determine whether to prosecute it to arbitration if ... a demand had been made upon it for such relief."[42]

Several Michigan cases are to the same effect. In *McGrail* v. *Detroit*

---

39. Id. at 574.
40. See, for example, Holodnak v. Avco Corp. and UAW Local 1010, 381 F. Supp. 191 (D. Conn. 1974), *aff'd in part and rev'd in part*, 514 F.2d 285 (2d Cir.), *cert. denied*, 423 U.S. 892 (1975).
41. 64 Misc.2d 524, 315 N.Y.S.2d 35 (Sup. Ct. 1970).
42. Id. at 532, 315 N.Y.S.2d at 44.

Federation of Teachers,[43] a substitute teacher filed a class action against the teachers' union and the board of education, alleging that they conspired to deny a pay raise to two classifications in their new collective bargaining agreement. In granting summary judgment for the defendants, the court, citing private sector precedents, declared that "absent a showing of bad faith, arbitrary or discriminatory action, or fraud, the union has complete discretion to negotiate contracts in the interest of the members as a whole."[44] In *Lowe* v. *Hotel & Restaurant Employees,*[45] however, the Michigan Supreme Court upheld a jury verdict in favor of an employee against his union representatives for a breach of the duty of fair representation. The employee had been discharged and the union had refused to process his grievance to arbitration. The court found that the evidence was sufficient for the jury to have concluded that the employee was wrongfully discharged, and that the union had made no effort to settle his grievance and had processed it in a "perfunctory manner."

Another interesting case — *Belanger* v. *Matteson*[46] — involved a conflict between two members of the same bargaining unit. The collective bargaining agreement under which they worked provided that when applicants for a vacancy had equal qualification, the most senior employee should be awarded the job. Although Matteson had more seniority, Belanger was initially granted the job; Matteson filed a grievance, which the union took to arbitration and won, thereby causing Belanger to be demoted to his former position. Belanger then filed a grievance, which the union refused to process. Belanger then sued the union. The trial court found that the union had breached its duty of fair representation; it vacated the award and reinstated Belanger. Matteson and the union appealed.

The Rhode Island Supreme Court, applying the duty of fair representation as developed by the federal courts in private sector cases, held that the union, by not considering fully the claims of both Belanger and Matteson before taking a position on the merits, had violated its duty of fair representation. In an approach that differs from that of the United States Supreme Court in *Hines,* the Rhode Island court pointed out that the employer had acted in good faith, having in fact vigorously argued in favor of Belanger at the hearing; that the arbitration was fair and regular; and that there was no reason in law why it should be vacated. It therefore reversed the lower court in respect of the vacatur of the arbitration award.

Thus, although it might be argued that the bargaining representa-

---

43. 82 LRRM 2623 (Mich. Cir. Ct. 1973); *accord,* Belen v. Woodbridge Bd. of Educ., 92 LRRM 3584 (N.J. Super. Ct. App. Div. 1976).
44. 82 LRRM 2623 at 2624.
45. 88 LRRM 3041 (Mich. Sup. Ct. 1973).
46. 346 A. 2d 124 (R.I. 1975), *cert. denied,* 424 U.S. 968 (1976).

tive's duty of fair representation should be enforced more strictly in the public than in the private sector, so far the courts have shown no inclination to do so. Further refinements in the law governing the duty of fair representation are likely to continue to be made in private sector cases and then adopted in the public sector.

Some Unresolved Questions

So much for the present state of the law of the union's duty of fair representation. What areas need clarification? What questions remain unanswered?

One of the most pressing questions is: exactly what types of conduct constitute a violation of the duty? On this point the Supreme Court has spoken with such impenetrable ambiguity that the federal courts, which bear the brunt of construing the nature and scope of the duty, are understandably in disagreement as to what the law is.

Let me briefly recapitulate the developments leading to the present confusion. The duty was defined as representation of "non-union or minority union members of the craft without hostile discrimination, fairly, impartially, and in good faith" in *Steele*.[47] In *Ford Motor Co.* v. *Huffman* the union's "wide range of reasonableness...in serving the unit it represents" was upheld, "subject always to complete good faith and honesty of purpose in the exercise of its discretion."[48] The Court refused to find a violation of the duty in *Humphrey* v. *Moore* in the absence of "substantial evidence of fraud, deceitful action or dishonest conduct."[49]

In *Vaca* v. *Sipes,* however, the Court introduced further elements in its consideration. A breach of the duty, it said, "occurs only when a union's conduct toward a member of the collective bargaining unit is *arbitrary,* discriminatory, or in bad faith."[50] It added that a union "may not arbitrarily ignore a meritorious grievance or process it in a *perfunctory* fashion."[51] In a dictum in *Amalgamated Association of Motor Coach Employes* v. *Lockridge,*[52] the Court said that to make out a claim of violation of the duty, an employee must have proved " 'arbitrary or bad-faith conduct on the part of the union.' There must be 'substantial evidence of fraud, deceitful action or dishonest conduct.' "[53] The Court thus combined the separate and by no means congruent definitions of a violation of the duty set forth

47. Steele v. Louisville & Nashville R.R., 323 U.S. 192 (1944) at 204.
48. 345 U.S. 330 (1953) at 338.
49. 375 U.S. 335 (1964) at 348.
50. 386 U.S. 171 at 190 (emphasis added).
51. Id. at 191 (emphasis added).
52. 403 U.S. 274 (1971).
53. Id. at 299.

in *Vaca* and in *Humphrey,* respectively, into a single, comprehensive definition.

Thereafter, confusion began to spread. In *Hines* v. *Anchor Motor Freight* the district court spoke of two standards: "bad faith or personal hostility,"[54] and "bad faith, arbitrariness or perfunctoriness."[55] The court of appeals referred to "bad faith or arbitrary conduct."[56] The Supreme Court's opinion quoted the early *Vaca* language; stated that Congress could not have intended to foreclose the employee from his Section 301 remedy "if the contractual processes have been seriously flawed by the union's breach of its duty to represent employees honestly and in good faith and without invidious discrimination or arbitrary conduct";[57] and implied that erroneous arbitration decisions should not stand when the employee's representation by the union has been "dishonest, in bad faith or discriminatory."[58]

Is it any wonder, then, that the federal circuit courts of appeals have defined a breach of the duty of fair representation in varying ways? To be specific, although the *Vaca* standard that a union violates the duty when it acts arbitrarily, discriminatorily, or in bad faith is universally applied in one form or another, the second circuit is the only court that requires a showing of bad faith before an action for breach of the duty can be brought.[59] Indeed, in *Jackson* v. *Trans World Airlines*[60] this test was narrowed to a required showing of hostile discrimination "akin to factual malice."[61]

The ninth circuit, on the other hand, has expressly rejected a required showing of bad faith. In *Beriault* v. *Local 40, ILWU,*[62] it concluded "that the district court applied an improper standard to the duty of fair representation when it found no breach of that duty solely because plaintiffs did not allege 'bad faith, deceitful or dishonest conduct on the part of the union.' "[63] The *Vaca* three-part test, it said, must be applied disjunctively: that is to say, a union violates the duty if its conduct is arbitrary, *or* discriminatory, *or* in bad faith. Three other circuits have also

---

54. Hines v. Local 377, Int'l Bhd. of Teamsters, 84 LRRM 2649 (N.D. Ohio 1973) at 2651.
55. Id. at 2650.
56. Hines v. Local 377, Int'l Bhd. of Teamsters, 506 F. 2d 1153 (6th Cir. 1974) at 1156.
57. 424 U.S. 554 at 570.
58. Id. at 571.
59. Simberlund v. Long Island R.R., 421 F.2d 1219 (2d Cir. 1970) at 1225; Cunningham v. Erie R.R., 266 F.2d 411 (2d Cir. 1959) at 417.
60. 67 CCH Lab. Cas. para. 12,546 (2d Cir. 1972).
61. Id. at para. 23,792.
62. 501 F.2d 258 (9th Cir. 1974).
63. Id. at 264.

concluded that proof of arbitrary conduct alone is sufficient to sustain a claim that a union violated its duty of fair representation.[64]

Although the Supreme Court has never dealt squarely with the question whether mere negligence on the union's part constitutes a breach of the duty of fair representation, there are a number of lower court decisions on this point. Several circuits have held that proof that a union may have acted negligently is not enough to support a claim of unfair representation,[65] and the NLRB has come to the same conclusion.[66] This view, however, is not unanimous. In *Holodnak* v. *Avco Corp. and UAW Local 1010*,[67] for example, the court based its judgment for the grievant-plaintiff in part on the finding that the union attorney representing the grievant in arbitration had overlooked obvious legal arguments and had not been sufficiently aggressive in protecting the grievant against improper questioning by the arbitrator.[68] In *Figueroa de Arroyo* v. *Sindicato de Trabajadores Packinghouse*,[69] the first circuit, although dismissing on other grounds a claim that the union had violated its duty of fair representation, found that evidence supporting the charge that the union had not investigated or made any judgment concerning the merits of the grievants' seniority claims, and had unwisely and inexplicably relied upon an NLRB proceeding to vindicate the grievants' unrelated contract rights was sufficient to support a finding that the duty had been violated. A federal district court in Virginia went even further in *Thompson* v. *International Association of Machinists, Lodge 1049*,[70] holding that the union violated its duty of fair representation by not giving notice to the grievant that his case was to be arbitrated; by not permitting him to be present at the arbitration, although knowing that no witnesses would be called to testify on his behalf; by investigating the grievance negligently and in a perfunctory manner; by taking an unsuccessful position in arbitration that was "doomed to failure"; and by failing to make a transcript of the hearing.

---

64. Sanderson v. Ford Motor Co., 483 F.2d 102 (5th Cir. 1973) at 110; Woods v. North American Rockwell Corp., 480 F.2d 644 (10th Cir. 1973) at 648; Griffin v. UAW, 469 F.2d 181 (4th Cir. 1972) at 183.

65. See, for example, Dente v. Masters, Mates & Pilots Local 90, 492 F.2d 10 (9th Cir. 1973); and Bazarte v. United Transp. Union, 429 F.2d 868 (3d Cir. 1970).

66. Local 18, Int'l Union of Operating Eng'rs (Ohio Pipe Line Constr. Co.), 144 NLRB 1365 (1963).

67. 381 F. Supp. 191 (D. Conn. 1974), *aff'd in part and rev'd in part*, 514 F.2d 285 (2d Cir.), *cert. denied*, 423 U.S. 892 (1975).

68. I have discussed this and other aspects of *Holodnak* in Benjamin Aaron, "The Impact of Public Employment Grievance Settlement on the Labor Arbitration Process," in American Arbitration Association, *The Future of Labor Arbitration in America* (New York: AAA, 1976), pp. 22–23.

69. 425 F.2d 281 (1st Cir.), *cert. denied*, 400 U.S. 877 (1970).

70. 258 F. Supp. 235 (E.D. Va. 1966).

Finally, the sixth circuit, in *Ruzicka* v. *General Motors,*[71] virtually obliterated any distinction between arbitrary and negligent conduct by holding on the basis of a finding that the union had negligently failed to file a grievance within the contractual time limits, that this negligence, "unrelated as it was to the merits of...[the grievant's] case," was "a clear example of arbitrary and perfunctory handling of a grievance."[72]

Whether these individual cases go too far, or not far enough, or strike a proper balance between the union's statutory right of exclusive representation and its duty of fair representation is, of course, a judgment about which opinions are bound to differ. Those decisions that have made no distinction between negligence and poor judgment[73] seem to me plainly wrong. Bad judgment is clearly distinguishable from negligence, and I can see no reason why employees should be entitled to a legally enforceable right to second-guess an unwise action by their statutory representative, in the absence of demonstrated bad faith.

Beyond that, however, the problem becomes somewhat stickier. Should arbitrary or negligent conduct be sufficient to constitute a breach of the duty? If by arbitrary we mean unreasonable, capricious, or perfunctory, I think it is a fair basis upon which to conclude that there has been a violation of the duty. About negligence, however, I am not so sure; the term is hardly a precise one and takes on different meanings in varying circumstances. It may on occasion carry no connotation of arbitrariness, discrimination, or bad faith — as when an overworked union steward inadvertently overlooks the deadline for filing an appeal from an adverse decision on a grievance to a higher step of the grievance procedure.

The proposition that a union must be found to have violated its duty of fair representation when its attorney falls short of the court's standards of competence by overlooking relevant legal arguments or pursuing those without merit is also troubling. In *Holodnak* there was some independent evidence to support a claim of bad faith on the union's part, but one can easily imagine a situation in which a lawyer, or more commonly, a union representative without legal training, simply does not know any better. For example, during the past few years I have arbitrated a large number of grievances—all involving discharges—for the same parties. In none of these cases has the union's position been even remotely vulnerable to a charge of bad faith, discrimination, or arbitrariness; yet in almost all of them the union's presentations, because of the lack of training and experience of its spokesmen, have been so inept as to prejudice the grievants' cases.

---

71. 523 F.2d 306 (6th Cir.), *rehearing denied,* 528 F.2d 912 (6th Cir. 1975).
72. Id. at 310.
73. See, for example, Bazarte v. United Transp. Union, 429 F.2d 868 (3d Cir. 1970).

As in most instances of a clash between two rights, it is necessary to strike a balance between the competing claims, and the manner in which those rights are balanced will depend very largely on the circumstances of the particular case. My own view is that a union ought not to be legally liable for a breach of its duty of fair representation unless its negligence is so gross as to indicate a reckless disregard of the grievant's rights.

On a related matter, I wholly agree with Professor David Feller that "the considerations applicable if the union has either failed to process an employee's grievance or settled it are quite different from those applicable if a union has pressed the claim before an impartial arbitrator and lost."[74] Professor Feller is concerned, as am I, that "judicial review of the quality of the union's representation could wreak havoc with a system the successful and economic operation of which requires both speed and reliance on nonlawyers."[75] The undesirable consequences of too intrusive a judicial review in these cases have been adumbrated in several of those previously mentioned. In each of them, the court's finding of a violation of the union's duty of fair representation was supported by the record as a whole. It would be improper, however, to reach such a conclusion *solely* because the union's attorney did not sufficiently protect the grievant from improper questioning by an arbitrator; or because in arbitration the union took an unsuccessful position that in the court's view was "doomed to failure"; or because the union did not have a transcript made of the arbitration proceedings.

A final problem that requires discussion concerns the status of grievance settlements reached by joint committees of union and management representatives without the participation of a neutral. Such arrangements are common in Teamster contracts and are also found in collective bargaining agreements in the airline industry. In the former, if no settlement is reached at the highest level of the hierarchy of joint committees to which successive appeals may be taken, the union is usually free to strike. In the latter, a neutral is typically called in to break the deadlock. Moreover, in at least some airline agreements, the individual grievant has the option of insisting that a neutral participate from the beginning.

The Supreme Court has consistently treated the decisions of joint committees as if they were no different from arbitration awards[76] and has concluded, therefore, that judicial review of such "awards" is limited by the principles laid down in *United Steelworkers* v. *Enterprise Wheel & Car*

---

74. David E. Feller, "A General Theory of the Collective Bargaining Agreement," *California Law Review* 61 (1973): 663, 812.
75. Ibid.
76. Hines v. Anchor Motor Freight, Inc., 424 U.S. 554 (1976); Humphrey v. Moore, 375 U.S. 335 (1964); Truck Drivers Local 89 v. Riss & Co., 372 U.S. 517 (1963).

Corp.[77] It seems obvious, however, that equating this procedure with arbitration is a mistake; in fact, settlements by a joint committee are no different from settlements reached at the final step of the grievance procedure preceding arbitration. Feller has pointed out the difference in these two views:

Treating decisions by joint committees as settlements made in the grievance procedure rather than as arbitration awards has at least two consequences. First, a decision is not subject to even the limited review for action in excess of jurisdiction to which arbitration awards are subject under *Enterprise*. Second, insofar as an individual's claim is concerned, a decision of a joint committee that his grievance lacks merit should bind him just as much, but no more, than a decision reached at the third or fourth step of a grievance procedure that the grievance should be abandoned, *i.e.*, settled on the basis of the company's answer at that step.[78]

Whether the decision of a joint committee is treated as an arbitration award or as a settlement reached in a grievance procedure, the problem for the individual grievant in proving a violation by the union of its duty of fair representation and in obtaining appropriate relief is a substantial one. This is especially so when the grievant is not a union member. Thus, the District of Columbia Circuit observed in *Edwards* v. *Capital Airlines*,[79] one of the early cases involving the union's duty of fair representation: "If the union were neutral in the dispute, that would be one thing. But where the union is aggressively presenting the interests of one group of employees and the company has no stake in the outcome, impartiality, protective of the rights of a nonmember minority, could hardly be conclusively presumed."[80]

On seniority issues the union's position cannot logically be neutral; it must, of necessity, support the views of one individual or group against those of another. The assumption always seems to be made, moreover, that the rights of the individual or group opposed by the union and favored by the employer are adequately represented and protected by the employer. I doubt if that is necessarily true. Surely, in *Edwards* the company could not have been expected to argue vigorously on behalf of two nonunion employees in an effort to achieve a result that would have caused dissatisfaction among the main body of employees, who were Air Line Pilots Association (ALPA) members. In the circumstances in *Belanger* v. *Matteson*, it seems to me that the court was right and that, at the very least, the union's duty of fair representation in a seniority case requires it to investigate the merits of the conflicting claims and to evaluate them in the light of the applicable provisions of the collective

---

77. 363 U.S. 593 (1960).
78. Feller, "A General Theory of the Collective Bargaining Agreement," p. 838.
79. 176 F.2d 755 (D.C. Cir.), *cert. denied*, 338 U.S. 885 (1949).
80. Id. at 760.

bargaining agreement and other pertinent considerations, if any, before deciding which side to support.

Cases such as *Edwards, Humphrey,* and *Hines* raise other complex questions. Should the individual employee, for example, have any independent rights to sue an employer for breach of a collective bargaining agreement, or should his remedy be confined to a suit against the union for breach of the duty of fair representation? If a bargaining agreement does not provide for arbitration, but permits the union to strike over grievances that remain unsettled after the grievance procedure has been exhausted, and if a grievant succeeds in proving that the union has violated its duty of fair representation in the processing of the grievance, to what remedy is the grievant then entitled?[81]

In conclusion, I hope I have made clear in this "overview" that in considering problems associated with the union's duty of fair representation the bird's-eye view of the courts is less revealing than the worm's-eye view of the individual employee from within a collective bargaining structure in which he has few if any independent rights.

---

81. These and related questions are exhaustively discussed in David Feller, "A General Theory of the Collective Bargaining Agreement."

The Origins of the Concept of the Duty of Fair Representation

James E. Jones, Jr.

It is commonplace to begin consideration of the duty of fair representation with a discussion of *Steele* v. *Louisville & Nashville Railroad.*[1] It is appropriate, therefore, to discuss how the duty originated before plunging into perceptions of where it has gone. At the time of the *Steele* case (around 1944) the duty of fair representation was a rather loose concept emerging from the necessity to deal with a concrete legal problem (union-management racial discrimination) without benefit of specific statutory authority, clear constitutional mandate, or explicit doctrinal analogies.

Consider, for example, the utilization of precedent by the Supreme Court in the *Steele* opinion: the Court cited no cases squarely in point for the proposition that the Constitution required the federal government to refrain from becoming involved in racial discrimination. For the proposition that Congress plainly did not undertake to authorize bargaining representatives to make racial discriminations, the Court cited *Yick Wo* v. *Hopkins,* 118 U.S. 356; *Yu Cong Eng* v. *Trinidad,* 271 U.S. 500; *Missouri Ex-rel Gaines* v. *Canada,* 305 U.S. 337; and *Hill* v. *Texas,* 316 U.S. 400. None of these cases is a Fifth Amendment case.[2] The concurring opinion,

---

1. 323 U.S. 192 (1944); see, for example, Neil M. Herring, "The Fair Representation Doctrine: An Effective Weapon against Union Racial Discrimination?" *Maryland Law Review* 24 (1964): 113; Charles J. Morris *et al., The Developing Labor Law* (Washington, D.C.: Bureau of National Affairs, 1971), chap. 27; Allan L. Bioff *et al., The Developing Labor Law Cumulative Supplement 1971–1975* (Washington, D.C.: Bureau of National Affairs, 1976), chap. 27; Robert A. Gorman, *The Basic Text on Labor Law* (St. Paul: West Publishing Co., 1976), chap. 30.

2. See 323 U.S. 192 at 203. It should be noted also that, in the celebrated case of Bolling v. Sharpe, 347 U.S. 497 (1954), which was the accompanying case to Brown v. Board of Educ., 347 U.S. 483 (1954) declaring separate-but-equal schools unconstitutional, the Supreme Court said, "As long ago as 1896, this Court declared the principle that the Constitution of the United States, in its present form, forbids, so far as civil and political rights are concerned, discrimination by the General Government, or by the States against any citizen because of his race." The Court relied upon Buchanan v. Warley, 245 U.S. 60 (1917), which held that a statute that limited the right of a property owner to convey his property to a person of another race was, as an unreasonable discrimination, a denial of due process of law. For this proposition the Warley Court cites Gibson v. Mississippi, 162 U.S. 565 and 591.

written by Justice Murphy, who wished to address the constitutional proposition squarely, cites no authority. For such a momentous decision these limited authorities are less than solid holdings on the proposition under consideration.

The economic and political climate of the country in 1944 had been substantially affected by World War II, during which America made great efforts to marshal psychological warfare on the racial issue in order "to make the world safe for democracy." Under the circumstances, perhaps it was more desirable for the Court to provide a basis for legal attack upon racial discrimination than for it to have strong precedents. It might also have been somewhat more politically expedient, given the demographic shifts that accompanied the country's substantial efforts to maintain a "guns and butter" economy.[3]

Once it had the *will* to decide the issue, the Court sought a rationale. As usual, arguments provided by advocates helped the Court reach the desired conclusions. In this case, Charles Hamilton Houston, the advocate for the black plaintiff, as well as the NAACP and the U.S. government, as *amicus curiae,* provided the Court with arguments.[4] The plaintiffs attempted to get the Court to declare the collective bargaining agreement between the unions and the railroads illegal; to state that a labor organization that refused on the basis of race to admit individuals in the craft or class to membership could not be a representative under the law; and to address these issues as constitutional questions. The Supreme Court did not go quite that far, but in view of the paucity of strong authorities on the constitutional claim, the Court's disposition of the matter was a rather far-reaching bit of judicial creativity. It phrased the issues as follows: "The question is whether the Railway Labor Act, 48 Stat. 1185, 45 U.S.C. §151 *et seq.,* imposes on the labor organization acting by authority of the statute as the exclusive bargaining representative of a craft or class of railway employees, the duty to represent all the employees in the craft without discrimination because of their race, and if so, whether the courts have jurisdiction to protect the minority of the craft or class from violation of such obligation."[5]

The Court ruled that it did. Comparing the union's role to that of a legislature, the Court stated:

---

3. For some descriptions of that period see Herbert Northrup, *Organized Labor and the Negro* (New York: Harper & Row, 1944); Louis Kesselman, *The Social Politics of FEPC* (Chapel Hill: University of North Carolina Press, 1948); and Robert Weaver, *Negro Labor* (New York: Harcourt Brace & Co., 1946).

4. See 89 L.Ed.2d 174–78 and 188–92 for summaries of arguments by counsel in respectively Steele v. Louisville & Nashville R.R., 323 U.S. 192 (1944), and in Tunstall v. Brotherhood of Locomotive Firemen & Enginemen, 323 U.S. 210 (1944).

5. 323 U.S. 192 at 193–94.

If as the state court has held, the Act conferred this power on the bargaining representative of a craft or class of employees without any commensurate statutory duty towards its members, constitutional questions arise. For the representative is clothed with power not unlike that of a legislature, which is subject to constitutional limitation on its power to deny, restrict, destroy or discriminate against the rights of those for whom it legislates, and which is also under an affirmative constitutional duty equally to protect those rights. If the Railway Labor Act purports to impose on petitioner and other Negro members of the craft the legal duty to comply with the terms of a contract whereby the representative has discriminatorily restricted their employment for the benefit and advantage of the Brotherhood's own members, we must decide the constitutional questions which petitioner raises in his pleading.

But we think that Congress, in enacting the Railway Labor Act and authorizing a union, chosen by majority of a craft, to represent the craft, did not intend to confer plenary power upon the union to sacrifice, for the benefit of its members, rights of the minority of the craft, without imposing on it any duty to protect the minority.[6]

Although, as the concurring opinion of Justice Murphy suggests, the Court's conclusion was propelled by a strong constitutional gloss, the majority found its mandate in the statute. As doctrine, however, and as a contribution to our search for the *origin* of this newly enunciated duty, the Court seemed to reach for broader, more basic concepts:

It is a principle of general application that the exercise of a granted power to act in behalf of others involves the assumption toward them of a duty to exercise the power in their interest and behalf, and that such a grant of power will not be deemed to dispense with all duty toward those for whom it is exercised unless so expressed.[7]

Although modern discussions of the nature of the duty of fair representation seem to focus upon the status of individuals under collective bargaining agreements, at least some observers recognize that the fundamental relationship harps back to general principles of trust law,[8] which, I submit, may be more comprehensive than a collective bargaining–contract theory of rights and obligations.

Professor Sanford Rosen observed in 1964 that:

The federal duty unquestionably is like a fiduciary obligation. As the United States Court of Appeals for the Fourth Circuit, in an opinion examining many of the significant decisions and articles on the subject, recently stated:

"Although the Supreme Court has not explicitly characterized this obligation by the very term 'fiduciary relationship,' its treatment of the subject is tantamount

---

6. Id. at 198–99.
7. Id. at 202.
8. See, for example, Sanford J. Rosen, "Fair Representation, Contract Breach and Fiduciary Obligations: Unions, Union Officials and the Worker in Collective Bargaining," *Hastings Law Journal* 15 (1963–64): 391 and references cited at 391–92, notes 1–9, and at 396, notes 21–23.

thereto. It has, in fact, said that 'Bargaining agents who enjoy the advantages of the Railway Labor Act's provisions *must execute their trust* without lawless invasions of the rights of other workers.'" While it is not always appropriate to transplant common law concepts to the field of labor relations, it is plain that in the Supreme Court's view, the federal statutory duty of fair representation is not unlike a common law fiduciary obligation.

To the same effect are major state court decisions examining the state common law or statutory duties of fair representation as well as the federal requirement.[9]

The foregoing observations suggest not only the fundamental nature of the duty of fair representation, but its origins in comfortable, common law concepts. If these observations are still apt, and I believe they are, then they suggest that as duty of fair representation cases proliferate in number and complexity, courts may take refuge from this double onslaught by *more explicit* adaptation of well-established trust law concepts to the emerging labor relations problems.

Although it may be as the fourth circuit opined in *Thompson* v. *Brotherhood of Sleeping Car Porters,*[10] that the Supreme Court had *behaved* as if the duty of fair representation were tantamount to the common law fiduciary obligation, I do not believe that the Supreme Court has said, "Go ye and look unto trust law for principles to apply when considering duty of fair representation cases." It did, however, make clear at the outset that the "extent and nature" of legal consequences of breach of the duty of fair representation were to be left to judicial determination.[11] Deciding these legal consequences required that the Court trace the metes and bounds of the duty of fair representation, and it is to those tracings I shall now briefly turn.

In *Tunstall* v. *Brotherhood of Locomotive Firemen and Enginemen,*[12] a companion case to *Steele,* the Court held that the duty of fair representation gave rise to a cause of action in the federal courts in a nondiversity case. The right asserted by the petition is derived from the duty imposed by the Railway Labor Act (RLA) on the union as representative of all employees in the craft or class. It is a federal right, implied from the

---

9. Id. at 398. Professor Rosen cites: Thompson v. Brotherhood of Sleeping Car Porters, 316 F.2d 191 (4th Cir. 1963) at 207; Charles Gregory, "Fiduciary Standards and the Bargaining and Grievance Process," *Labor Law Journal* 8(1957): 843; Jenkins v. William Schluderberg — T. J. Kurdle Co., 217 Md. 556, 564–65, 574–75; 144 A. 2d 88, 93, 98–99 (1958); Clark v. Hein-Werner Corp., 8 Wis.2d 264, 99 N.W.2d 132 (1959); *rehearing denied,* 8 Wis.2d 264, 100 N.W.2d 317 (1960), *cert. denied,* 362 U.S. 962 (1960); Falsetti v. Local No. 2026 UMW, 400 Pa. 145, 171–72, 161 A.2d 882 (1960) at 895–96. See Archibald Cox, "Rights under a Labor Agreement," *Harvard Law Review* 69(1956): 601, 645–46, 652; Archibald Cox, "Individual Enforcement of Collective Bargaining Agreements," *Labor Law Journal* 8(1957): 850, 853–54.
10. 316 F.2d 191 at 207.
11. See 323 U.S. 204 (1944).
12. 323 U.S. 210.

federal statutes, that condemns the discriminatory conduct of the union as unlawful.[13]

One of the least noted decisions on the duty of fair representation was handed down by the Supreme Court on the same day it decided *Steele* and *Tunstall*. Without citing either of those cases, the Court applied the duty of fair representation in *Wallace Corp.* v. *National Labor Relations Board*[14] to unions operating under the National Labor Relations Act (NLRA) in a nonrace case. *Wallace* involved efforts of a union, unlawfully established, maintained, or assisted by an employer, to bring about the discharge of employees who had supported its rival, which had lost the election. Even though a closed shop was not illegal under federal law at that time, the Supreme Court agreed with the National Labor Relations Board (NLRB) that enforcement of the closed shop requiring union membership—a requirement the victorious union intended to deny to its rival—was an unfair labor practice contrary to section 8(3) of the law. The Court said:

The duties of a bargaining agent selected under the terms of the Act extend beyond the mere representation of the interests of its own group members. By its selection as bargaining representative, it has become the *agent* of all the employees *charged with the responsibility of representing their interests fairly and impartially.* . . . We do not construe the provision [of the National Labor Relations Act] authorizing a closed shop contract as indicating an intention of Congress to authorize a majority of the workers and the company, as in the instant case, to penalize minority groups of workers by depriving them of that full freedom of association and self-organization which it was the prime purpose of the Act to protect for all workers.[15]

In *Wallace,* therefore, not only does the Court extend the duty of fair representation to unions under the NLRA but it expands that duty beyond *invidious* racial discrimination.[16] It also seems to invoke concepts of *agency* to describe the affirmative obligation the union owed by virtue of its statutory position.

Thus, the earliest Supreme Court cases on the emerging duty of fair representation refer to concepts of agency and suggest fiduciary obligations under trust law. The nonconstitutional sources of the obligation and the nonracial aspects of the duty of fair representation both seem to have been neglected for several years. So, too, did the utilization of the NLRA's unfair labor practice provisions as a statutory basis for dealing with breaches of the duty of fair representation.[17]

---

13. Id. at 213.

14. 323 U.S. 248 (1944).

15. Id. at 255–56 (emphasis added).

16. The Court agreed with the Board that the union-induced breach of the employer's statutory duty under sections 8(2) and 8(3) violated the union's duty of fair representation. There were no union unfair labor practices under the law at that time.

17. See Archibald Cox, "The Duty of Fair Representation," *Villanova Law Review* 2(1957): 151; Miranda Fuel Co., 140 NLRB 181 (1962), *enforcement denied*, 326 F.2d 172 (2d Cir. 1963); Hughes Tool Co., 147 NLRB 1573 (1964).

The New Scope of the Duty of Fair Representation

Subsequent to 1944, major cases began to outline this new duty, trying to specify which kinds of conduct or labor union activities were included within the duty owing.[18] In *Betts* v. *Easley*,[19] for example, the Supreme Court of Kansas demonstrated the creative use, or misuse as strict constructionists would no doubt label it, of the *Steele* doctrine by supplying a near contemporaneous example of the potential, substantive scope of the duty of fair representation. The term *substantive* is used here to mean the kinds of trade union activities and functions that would be subject to the duty enunciated in *Steele* as distinguished from the care or lack thereof with which the labor union might carry out those duties. As you will recall, *Steele* and *Tunstall* dealt with the *making* of a collective agreement. One could anticipate that lawyers would assert in future litigation that the act of negotiating the agreement was the sum total of the duty. The Kansas Supreme Court in *Betts* took on the entire range of duties involved in fairly representing members of the class and, except for the purely social activities, decreed that blacks had the enforceable right to participate. The court noted:

To what extent the union may lawfully segregate its membership on the basis of race, color, or any other basis it chooses, in connection solely with local activities which are wholly independent of its functions as the designated collective bargaining agent is a question not before us. We are concerned here with segregation which carries with it alleged inequality of participation in union affairs relating to hours, wages, grievances, working conditions and other such important matters incident to employment, which are within the scope of negotiation and settlement under the Railway Labor Act.[20]

The primary question before the Kansas court was whether or not the collective bargaining agent for all the workers could lawfully exclude eligible Negro workers from full participation in privileges incident to the Act and admit them to membership only in a separate lodge, which would be under the jurisdiction of and represented by the delegates of the nearest white local. Under existing conditions the black local was not permitted to transact its own business; Negro workers were not permitted to attend the white meetings or to vote on the election of officers or on anything pertaining to the business of the local lodge; they could not participate in determining policy, vote on questions of dues, or help select those who would represent them; and they could not be delegates in any meetings or conventions. In addition to requesting that the provisions of the constitution and bylaws of the labor organization that required this racial separation be declared null and void, the plaintiffs requested that the union be prohibited from acting as the bargaining agent for any individuals under the Railway Labor Act until such time as the Negro members were given equality of privileges and participation in the affairs of the labor organization.

The Kansas court found the practices of the labor organization to be in violation of the Railway Labor Act, Kansas law, and the Fifth and Fourteenth Amendments of the U.S. Constitution. Contrary to the careful avoidance of the constitutional issues by Justice Stone for the United States Supreme Court in *Steele,* the Kansas court converted the *Steele* opinion into a precedent of constitutional law and applied it comprehensively. Although the technical issue of membership might not have been before the Kansas court since blacks were members of the union though relegated to separate local lodges, it is doubtful that that difference between the facts of *Betts* and *Steele* would have made the slightest difference to the Kansas court. It asserts in one place, "Mere technical arguments, which disregard reality, speak with feeble force when basic freedoms are jeopardized." In the process of resolving the issues before it, the Kansas court uses *Steele* more as an axe than as a scalpel. *Betts* v. *Easley,* which was generally ignored as precedent for twenty years, was either bad law or a concept that was too far ahead of its time.

In sum, with regard to the identity of those persons or classes of persons entitled by right to the duty of fair representation, *Steele* and *Tunstall* make clear that members of the craft or class, though excluded from union membership, ought to be protected from racial discrimination. *Wallace* adds protection for persons in the unit (NLRA counterpart of craft or class) who are excluded from the union for political reasons. While *Steele* and *Tunstall* involve seniority rights, job preferences, layoffs, and recall, *Wallace* involves protection from discharge.

Probably the most startling development of the duty of fair representation was in the *Brotherhood of Railroad Trainmen* v. *Howard.*[21] Unlike *Steele,* the petitioners in *Howard* were not members of the same craft or class as represented by the defendant union. The Brotherhood of Railroad Trainmen, which represented white brakemen, negotiated a collective bargaining agreement with the railroad to take over the jobs of train porters—black jobs represented by another union. The jobs differed in that train porters, in addition to doing everything that brakemen did, were also required to sweep the coaches and to assist passengers in getting on and off the train.[22]

In their decision in *Howard* the Supreme Court said: "Bargaining agents who enjoy the advantage of the Railway Labor Act's provisions

---

21. 343 U.S. 768 (1952).
22. Id. at 771, note 3.

must exercise their trust without lawless invasion of the rights of other workers." Substantial flexibility was thus given the district courts in deriving a decree to protect these employees from future discrimination, but recognizing that disputes over "craft or class" were matters committed to the National Mediation Board.

It is not clear if only *invidious* racial discrimination calls forth this expansive interpretation of the scope of the duty of fair representation. Certainly, a respectable argument of limitation can be made. Conceptually, however, the case established that in addition to the duty to represent all in its constituency fairly, a union has the duty to exercise its trust without lawless invasion of the rights of others whom it was not selected to serve.

One would think that after such an expansive reading of the scope of the duty of fair representation at a minimum parties would subsequently conceive of the duty as coextensive with their powers and functions. Not so. In 1957 the Supreme Court heard *Conley* v. *Gibson*.[23] In this case the company had purported to abolish forty-five jobs held by black workers who were discharged or demoted; instead, it gave the jobs to white workers. The blacks complained, but the union refused to process their grievances. There were two facts of significance in this case: (1) the blacks were members of the craft or class *and* members of the union; and (2) the dispute was over the failure or refusal of the union to process the petitioners' grievances under a collective bargaining agreement. Justice Black for the Supreme Court said:

Once again, Negro employees are here under the Railway Labor Act asking that their collective bargaining agent be compelled to represent them fairly.

...This Court squarely held in *Steele* and subsequent cases that discrimination in representation because of race is prohibited by the Railway Labor Act. The bargaining representative's duty not to draw "irrelevant and invidious" distinctions among those it represents does not come to an abrupt end, as the respondents seem to contend, with the making of an agreement between union and employer. Collective bargaining is a continuous process. Among other things, it involves day-to-day adjustments in the contract and other working rules, resolution of new problems not covered by existing agreements, and the protection of employee rights already secured by contract. The bargaining representative can no more unfairly discriminate in carrying out these functions than it can in negotiating a collective agreement. A contract may be fair and impartial on its face yet administered in such a way with the *active* or *tacit consent of the union*, as to be flagrantly discriminatory against some members of the bargaining unit.[24]

The Court, furthermore, cited with approval *Hughes Tool Co.* v. *National Labor Relations Board*, 147 F. 2d 69 (5th Cir. 1945) at 74, for the proposition

23. 355 U.S. 41 (1957).
24. Id. at 42 and 46 (emphasis added).

that the union's duty of fair representation also included the grievance process, thus making it clear that the principle applied in *Conley* v. *Gibson* was also applicable to unions operating under the NLRA.[25]

It seems fair to say that by 1957 it was clear that the duty of fair representation was coextensive with the union's collective bargaining functions under the statutes, but the problem addressed in *Betts* v. *Easley* —namely, the entitlement of the black to full membership and participation—was still unresolved. The demise of the separate-but-equal doctrine as constitutional[26] preceded by some time the demise of the constitutionality of separate-but-equal in the practices of labor unions under the labor relations laws.[27]

It should be noted that on the sticky issue of membership the U.S. Court of Appeals for the Sixth Circuit declined to read *Steele,* either under a statutory interpretation or under a separate-but-equal doctrine, as entitling black petitioners to admission to union membership. In *Oliphant* v. *Brotherhood of Locomotive Firemen and Engineers*[28] — even after *Brown* v. *Board of Education* and *Bolling* v. *Sharpe*—the court declined to go that far, and the Supreme Court declined to review the matter, saying: "In view of the abstract context in which the question sought to be raised is presented by this record, the petition for writ for *certiorari* to the U.S. Court of Appeals for the Sixth Circuit is denied."[29] That opinion chilled the hopes of civil rights advocates regarding the continued viability of the duty of fair representation as a device to integrate unions against their will.

The Fairness Issue

The illustrations so far have concentrated on the question of *representation* and on probing the aspects of the duties which were included within the concept. The question of *fairness* received scant attention from the judiciary. Small wonder at this paucity of judicial attention since the unfairness involved in the major cases was so gross. It was easy to identify the hostile, invidious discrimination in the refusals or failures of the unions to act at all or in the affirmative actions they took to injure others. Identifying the acts was a simple process by comparison to attempting to

---

25. Id. at 46, note 7. In Syres v. Oil Workers Int'l Union, 350 U.S. 892 (1955), any doubt as to the applicability of the Steele doctrine to cases arising under the NLRA was removed in a *per curiam* opinion.

26. Brown v. Board of Educ., 347 U.S. 483 (1954); Bolling v. Sharpe, 347 U.S. 497 (1954).

27. See Hughes Tool Co., *supra* footnote 17. But also see Handy Andy, Inc., 228 NLRB 59 (1977).

28. 262 F.2d 359 (6th Cir. 1958).

29. 359 U.S. 935, *rehearing denied,* 359 U.S. 962 (1959).

evaluate the *reasonableness* of the decisions to act or not to act or the quality of the actions taken by the union trustee.

Ford v. *Huffman*[30] started the Court down the road of inquiry that appears to have replaced race and other invidious discrimination as the focus of recent duty of fair representation cases. The *Ford* case involved a collective bargaining provision between the company and the United Automobile Workers which, after six months of probationary employment, gave pre-employment seniority credit to veterans for time spent in the post-1941 military. The statute (50 U.S.C. App. Section 308 (b)(B), 54 Stat. 890, 58 Stat. 798) already required returning veterans to be put into their rightful places. This early case of fictional seniority was challenged as invalid under the Selective Training and Service Act of 1940 and in excess of the union's authority as bargaining representative. The Supreme Court disagreed. In upholding the collective bargaining agreement it reiterated the duty of fair representation and enunciated an affirmative standard of conduct for unions:

... That the authority of bargaining representatives, however, is not absolute is recognized in Steele v. Louisville N. R. Co., 323 U.S. 192, 198–199 in connection with comparable provisions of the Railway Labor Act. Their statutory obligations to represent all members of an appropriate unit requires them to make an honest effort to serve the interests of all those members, without hostility to any. *Id.* at 198, 202–204; Tunstall v. Brotherhood of Locomotive Firemen & Enginemen, 323 U.S. 210, 211; Brotherhood of Railroad Trainmen v. Howard, 343 U.S. 768. ...Inevitably, differences arise in the manner and degree to which the terms of any negotiated agreement affect individual employees and classes of employees. The mere existence of such differences does not make them invalid. The complete satisfaction of all who are represented is hardly to be expected. *A wide range of reasonableness must be allowed a statutory bargaining representative in serving the unit it represents, subject always to complete good faith and honesty of purpose in the exercise of its discretion.*[31]

This line of cases indicates clearly that something more than a lack of hostility is required in order for the duty of fair representation to be appropriately discharged. Honest effort, good faith, and honesty of purpose in the exercise of discretion emerge as standards of union conduct. A wide range of reasonableness obviously implies at least a narrow margin of intolerable unreasonableness, bringing into the judicial calculus a different level of consideration than was previously implied in terms like good faith and honesty.

The discussion of *Ford* v. *Huffman* (1952) is presented out of chronological sequence, because the case is prophetic; it suggests the

---

30. 345 U.S. 330 (1953).
31. Id. at 337–38 (emphasis added).

necessity for unions to strike a balance between legitimate interests and implicit standards to be applied in evaluating any such balance. The case is significantly different from prior cases in that it suggests the beginnings of the evaluation of the *quality* of the union's performance of its duty to its members. This more generalized concern with the quality of the performance of the representation function remains important today.

Events between the *Oliphant* decision of 1959 and *Humphrey* v. *Moore*[32] in 1964 substantially overtook the duty of fair representation doctrine as a vehicle for dealing with racial discrimination and substituted, arguably, more direct and efficient methods for dealing with its corrupting and overriding influence. Without the background of employment discrimination matters, including union membership, it is easier to probe the duty of fair representation as that of a trustee charged with the welfare of his wards, rather than as a constitutional shield against deliberate, invidious abuse by the bargaining representative of some of the persons committed to its charge. With the elimination of the corrupting and overriding influence of racial discrimination, it will be easier for the courts to turn their attention to the plight of individual workers as they contend with their union institutions over the quality of the performance of the unions' trust obligations.

Recall, if you will, this nation's inability directly to address the issue of racial exclusion. This inability corrupted the decision in *Steele* and all its progeny except perhaps *Betts* v. *Easley* and gave an unnatural quality to the theory of the duty of fair representation. That unnatural quality placed the union under an obligation to treat all those it was by law authorized to represent in a manner free of hostile and invidious discrimination. But the same theory permitted that union totally to exclude certain individuals in its constituency from any participation in the collective bargaining process, or the process of union governance, particularly from membership in and access to any of the internal political processes. The excluded persons were accorded access to the courts, however, to ensure that the "other" obligations of fair representation were fairly honored. The freedom of association and collective action in *Wallace* was not to be confused with the right to be in and take part. Nor were the individuals free to pursue their separate ways and make independent deals.

The Labor Management Reporting and Disclosure Act (LMRDA), passed by Congress in 1959, includes an extensive list of rights with regard to internal union affairs and, either explicitly or implicitly, reaches all phases of union activity including collective bargaining agreements

---

32. 379 U.S. 335 (1964).

and duty of fair representation issues, at least to the extent that the law incorporates the constitution, bylaws, and procedures of unions.[33]

The continuation in 1959 of the corruptive influence of race is to be noted in passing. Most conceivable trade union obligations found some protection in the Landrum-Griffin Act *except* for racial discrimination by omission and communist affiliation by specific exclusion.[34]

It is ironic that on July 1, 1964, the NLRB issued its decision in the *Hughes Tool* case,[35] and the next day Congress passed the Civil Rights Act. Each governmental action spoke to the issue of racial discrimination by unions. The *Hughes Tool* case outlined in its footnote references evidence of the march of the law which made that decision possible — *Shelley* v. *Kraemer*, 334 U.S. 1 (1948); *Hurd* v. *Hodge*, 334 U.S. 224 (1948); *Brown* v. *Board of Education*, 347 U.S. 483 (1954); *Bolling* v. *Sharpe*, 347 U.S. 497 (1954); and, additionally, *Steele, Tunstall,* and *Wallace* mentioned earlier. The NLRB and trial examiner Fred U. Reel used their statute to make the breach of the duty of fair representation — not just invidious racial discrimination but other *arbitrary* or irrational discrimination, too — an unfair labor practice.[36]

These twin acts of July 1964 made possible a much broader exploration of the duty of fair representation issues than before, for they directly addressed racial exclusion from membership and from any other union-connected or work-connected activity. It is no longer necessary to strain to find a way to deal with racial segregation. The system is now much freer to look closely at the noninvidious behavior of unions and to examine this behavior as a matter of the general duty owed to those the union is charged with representing fairly.

Since 1964 only one principal case involving race has, to my knowledge, reached the Supreme Court under the duty of fair representation theory: *Glover* v. *St. Louis & San Francisco Railroad.*[37] This is probably due

---

33. Section 105(a)(5) of Title II of the Labor-Management Reporting and Disclosure Act, 29 U.S.C. § 431(a)(5) (1959). Additionally, Title V of the act, particularly section 501(a), arguably, covers every part of the union's activities. The fiduciary obligation on its face, and to some extent in its legislative history, is broad enough to reach more than the mere handling of union property and union money. Moreover, section 302, regulating union trusteeships, sets forth in rather broad language the legitimate functions of the trusteeship. It speaks to some of the more basic obligations of unions such as "assuring the performance of collective bargaining agreements *or other duties of a bargaining representative,* restoring democratic procedures, or otherwise carrying out the legitimate objects of such labor organization" (emphasis added). Pub. L. 86-257, Title III, § 302, Sept. 14, 1959, 73 Stat. 531; 29 U.S.C. § 462.

34. 29 U.S.C. § 504, but see U.S. v. Brown, 381 U.S. 437 (1965) declaring that provision prohibiting a member of the Communist party to hold office unconstitutional.

35. *Supra* footnote 17.

36. See also Miranda Fuel, *supra* footnote 17; Jubilee Mfg. Co., 202 NLRB 272 (1973), enf'd *per curiam,* 87 LRRM 3168, 75 CCH Lab. Cas. 10,405 (D.C. Cir. 1974).

37. 393 U.S. 324 (1969).

to the fact that now, particularly in the face of the availability of Title VII and of 42 U.S.C. 1981,[38] there is little basis for bringing a race case under the duty of fair representation theory. *Glover* is significant, however, in that the Supreme Court pointed out (after *Vaca* v. *Sipes*[39] and *Republic Steel Corp.* v. *Maddox*[40]) that the exhaustion requirement was subject to a number of exceptions. The *futility* exception was of sufficient force to apply to any remedy administered by the union, by the company, or both, to pass upon the claims of the employees whose rights they had been charged with neglecting and betraying.

In view of these decisions, it would be surprising to see future Supreme Court cases on the racial discrimination issue under the duty of fair representation. That then leaves the doctrine available to perform some other service. The prime candidate for that is the collective bargaining process.

Quality of Performance

Recent Supreme Court cases, beginning with *Humphrey* v. *Moore,* 375 U.S. 335 (1964), and ending with *Hines* v. *Anchor Motor Freight, Inc.,* 424 U.S. 554 (96 S. Ct. 1048 [1976]), mark a period of judicial preoccupation with aspects of the duty of fair representation heretofore neglected or under-emphasized — the concern with *quality* of the performance of the duty rather than its scope or content. For analytical purposes, this might be labeled as concern with the procedural mechanics of the duty performed rather than its scope or substantive aspects.

Of no particular chronological significance, but typical of many contemporary instruments specifically directed toward dealing with racial discrimination, is the 1964 *Humphrey* v. *Moore* case. This case involves allegations against the union of dishonest conduct in breach of its duty of fair representation, deceiving one group of employees while conniving with another to deprive the former of seniority rights, and preventing the grievants from obtaining a fair hearing. Moreover, it was claimed that the bipartite tribunal exceeded the authority granted it to deal with the grievance in question.

Without getting into the Court's confusion as to the nature of the cause of action,[41] it is sufficient for our purposes to note that the petition-

---

38. See, for example, Jones v. Alfred H. Mayer Co., 392 U.S. 409, 441–43 at note 78 (1968).

39. 386 U.S. 171 (1967).

40. 379 U.S. 650 (1965).

41. The majority opinion found that jurisdiction existed under § 301 of the LMRA, 29 U.S.C. § 185, 375 U.S. 335 at 343–44, while Goldberg concurring in the result of reversal reasoned that Moore's claim derived not from the collective bargaining agreement, but from the union's statutory duty of fair representation. 375 U.S. 335 at 351–59.

ers succeeded in getting judicial oversight of (1) the authority of a bipartite collective bargaining mechanism to address itself to the conflict in question in the first place; (2) the capacity of the union to represent employees whose interests were directly in conflict (the merger of seniority lines obviously required some employees to lose and some to gain, and the union represented them both); (3) whether mistaken, bad advice would be converted to deceitful or fraudulent behavior; and (4) whether the timing and availability of new information compromised the ability of the complainants to get a fair hearing. This fair hearing aspect was clearly a procedural due process issue.

The court found that these allegations raised the issue of the union's breach of its duty of fair representation. After examination of the facts, it concluded that the union had not breached its duty, but had taken its position honestly, in good faith, and without hostile or arbitrary discrimination; that the lateness of notification that the union was going to oppose one group's interest did not deprive its members of a fair hearing or adequate representation; that neither the union nor the company, who were parties to the joint committee, exceeded their power under the contract; and that there was no fraud or breach of the duty by the exclusive bargaining agent.

The significance of this case for predicting future trends is the willingness of the courts to look very closely at procedural practices and at the questions of conflict of interest and of action in excess of contractual authority. It is in this area of scope of authority to resolve a disputed issue that future controversy might arise. It also seems significant for the future that the court is willing to evaluate union conduct by a variety of normative standards. Terms emerged in this case on the scope of authority and issues of "fraud and deprivation of a fair hearing by virtue of inadequate representation at such hearing." The Court also found that the union acted honestly, in good faith, and without hostility or *arbitrary* discrimination; that the union acted upon *wholly relevant considerations, not upon capricious or arbitrary factors.* In the search by advocates and lower courts for guidance in applying the slippery dimensions of the duty of fair representation, these terms with their suggestions of norms will obviously receive continued attention.

Another case, *Republic Steel Corp.* v. *Maddox,*[42] contributes procedurally to our understanding the duty of fair representation by making clear that if there is a collective bargaining process, before resorting to the courts on a breach of contract theory, one has to resort to the contractual provisions. In other words, the exhaustion of the available administrative agencies concept is applicable even in a case where the employment re-

42. 379 U.S. 650 (1965).

lationship may be said to have been permanently severed. It would seem that breach of contract–duty of fair representation actions may be barred if the party seeking judicial relief has not made an effort to exhaust the available contractual remedy. There may be at least one continuing important exception to this proposition and that is the racial discrimination futility exception, which the Supreme Court noted subsequent to *Republic Steel* in *Glover* v. *St. Louis & San Francisco Railroad.*

Vaca v. *Sipes*,[43] by inference, blessed the NLRB's tardy assumption of unfair labor practice jurisdiction for breaches of the duty of fair representation, but made clear that such assumption did not oust the courts of their traditional jurisdiction over fair representation cases that was judicially developed. In addition, it reinforced what had already started to emerge as the arbitrary conduct norm in *Humphrey* v. *Moore*. The Court said:

A breach of the statutory duty of fair representation occurs only when a union's conduct toward a member of the collective bargaining unit is arbitrary, discriminatory, or in bad faith.... Though we accept the proposition that a union may not *arbitrarily ignore a meritorious grievance or process it in a perfunctory fashion,* we do not agree that the individual employee has an absolute right to have his grievance taken to arbitration regardless of the provisions of the applicable collective bargaining agreement.

The case also makes clear that the fact that another tribunal may decide that a grievance had merit where the union had decided contrarily does not necessarily provide the basis for breach of the duty of fair representation. When the union makes its decision on the merits of the case and in a good-faith and nonarbitrary manner, breach of the duty of fair representation is not established merely by proof that the grievance was meritorious. The Court notes, however, that if an individual supplied the union with evidence supporting his position, the union might well breach its duty if it ignored the employee's complaint or processed the grievance in a perfunctory manner. Although in the case in point the union was held not to have breached its duty, in the process the Supreme Court reemphasized arbitrariness-nonarbitrariness as a standard of reviewing union conduct and added another one, the perfunctory processing of the grievance.

It is difficult to tell whether the next pertinent case, *Amalgamated Association of Street, Electric Railway & Motor Coach Employes of America* v. *Lockridge*,[44] will expand or contract the concept of the duty of fair representation. In it the Court states that for such a claim (a breach of the duty of fair representation) to be made out, Lockridge must have proved

43. 386 U.S. 171 (1967) (quoted wording at 190–91, emphasis added).
44. 403 U.S. 274 (1971).

"arbitrary or bad faith conduct on the part of the union" as in *Vaca* v. *Sipes* and "substantial evidence of fraud, deceitful action or dishonest conduct" as in *Humphrey* v. *Moore.* It states further that the distinction between honest, mistaken conduct, on the one hand, and deliberate and severely hostile and irrational treatment, on the other, needs strictly to be maintained.[45] It also notes that breach of the duty of fair representation must be established by "substantial evidence of discrimination that is intentional, severe, and unrelated to legitimate union objectives."[46] An obvious area of litigation is open for the future to determine what facts will be necessary or sufficient to meet these standards.[47]

One other Supreme Court case — *Hines* v. *Anchor Motor Freight*[48] — deals with the issue of whether it was appropriate to dismiss a cause of action against an employer by employees asserting a breach of the collective bargaining contract where an accompanying complaint against the unions for breach of the duty of fair representation had withstood a motion for summary judgment and had been sent back for trial.

The employees had been discharged by the employer for alleged dishonesty. The union, claiming that the employees were innocent, had taken the matter to arbitration to a bipartite committee where the discharges were upheld. Subsequently, information indicating the charges of dishonesty had been false came out. In an investigation by an attorney in connection with the lawsuit, a deposition of a motel clerk revealed falsification of records for which the employees had been discharged. It had been alleged that the falsity of the charges could have been uncovered with a minimum of investigation by the union and that the union had made no effort to ascertain the truth and had thereby violated its duty of fair representation. Despite this, the district court granted a motion for summary judgment for both the union and the employer, concluding that the arbitration committee's decision was final and binding on the employees and that they had failed to show facts comprising bad faith, arbitrariness, or perfunctoriness on the part of the union. The district court opined that the act of the union might not have met professional standards of competency, and it might have been advisable for the union to have further investigated the case, but that these factors demonstrated bad judgment at most and were insufficient to prove breach of the duty of fair representation.

On reviewing the matter, the court of appeals concluded that the facts were sufficient to support an inference of bad faith or arbitrary

---

45. Id. at 301.
46. Id.
47. See, for example, Trail v. International Bhd. of Teamsters, 542 F.2d 961 (6th Cir. 1976).
48. 424 U.S. 554, 96 S. Ct. 1048 (1976).

conduct and the petitioners should have had an opportunity to have a trial on their charges.[49] The court of appeals dismissed with respect to the employer, however, on the theory that there was no evidence of any misconduct on the employer's part and wholly insufficient evidence of any conspiracy between the union and the employer.[50] It was on this issue that the Supreme Court reversed the court below. It opined that the employer need not be implicated in the bad faith or misconduct of the union in order to be liable for breach of contract.

In my judgment, however, that is not the most significant aspect of *Hines* for future duty of fair representation issues. More significantly, it seems to me, is the determination of the court of appeals which was not upset by the Supreme Court. The charges made by the union members were sufficient to go to trial on the issue of breach of the duty of fair representation. Those charges were as follows:

They consist of the motel clerk's admission, made a year after the discharge was upheld in the arbitration, that he, not the plaintiffs, pocketed the money; the claim of the union's failure to investigate the motel clerk's original story implicating plaintiffs despite their request; the account of the union officials' assurance to the plaintiffs that they had nothing to worry about, that there was no need for them to investigate; the contention that no exculpatory evidence was presented at the hearing; and the assertion that there existed political antagonisms between local union officials and plaintiffs because of a wildcat strike, led by some of the plaintiffs and the dispute over the appointment of a steward, resulting in denunciation of plaintiffs as "hillbillies" by Angelo, the union president.[51]

The Supreme Court in *Hines* makes clear that "the union's breach of duty relieves the employee of an express or implied requirement that disputes be settled through contractual grievance procedures; if it seriously undermines the integrity of the arbitral process, the union's breach also removes the bar of the finality provision of the contract."[52] The Supreme Court repeats that in *Vaca* it had accepted the proposition that a union might not arbitrarily ignore a meritorious grievance or process it in a perfunctory fashion, and that its determination in that case that the union had not breached its duty of fair representation was based upon the Court's evaluation of the *manner* in which the union had handled the grievance in its earlier stages.

What seems to me on trial in this case is a judicial evaluation of the *manner* in which the union conducted the arbitration. Terms like "arbitrary, capricious, perfunctory" and inquiries into "whether the employer knowingly or negligently relied on false evidence" and whether the employer is implicated in the union's *malfeasance* all bring us closer to

49. 506 F.2d 1153 (6th Cir. 1974).
50. Id. at 1157–58.
51. Id. at 1156.
52. 96 S. Ct. 1048 at 1058.

considerations of negligence as a standard by which union behavior will be evaluated. It is, of course, much easier for the courts to borrow well-established concepts such as reasonable care and rational basis than to create new content for less well developed concepts like "perfunctory," "fairly," and "in good faith."

Conclusion

This paper is intended to be a think piece rather than an exhaustive analysis of the problems involved in the duty of fair representation. An exhaustive discussion would have to trace developments of trust and fiduciary concepts as well as the nature of labor organizations.[53] Such a discussion would also seem required to explore just what "rights, powers and duties" are[54] and the question, "Can equity then create such rights as it finds to be necessary for the purposes of justice?" I suggest for future research just such a "conceptual" exploration. For the purposes of this paper, however, the observations developed must suffice.

In the march of law from the emergence of the duty of fair representation to perhaps the mid-1960s, the concept was stunted in its full development by the overriding preoccupation in the cases with the racial discrimination issue and particularly with the difficulty in overcoming what seemed to be statutory approval of exclusion of blacks or separation of blacks from union participation.

It has been suggested that while constitutional necessity was used as the fundamental premise in the *Steele* case for the *imposition* of the duty of fair representation, it was not the constitutional dimension that determined the substantive and procedural content of the concept. It was a broader dimension involved in the common law of trusts and of fiduciary obligatons. While it is a much more limited notion to erect a constitution as a shield against invidious or hostile conduct, or even as a fundamental requirement for equal treatment, the law of fiduciary relationships imposes upon the guardian a much broader responsibility to undertake to protect the interests of his wards.

It is this idea that remained submerged in the duty of fair representation for an extended period of time because of the corrupting influence of

---

53. See, for example, on this latter issue alone: Zechariah Chafee, "The Internal Affairs of Associations Not for Profit," *Harvard Law Review* 43(1930): 993, in which he counters earlier arguments of the necessity for legislative authorization before groups can have legal rights, powers, and duties (see p. 1009, note 44).

54. This question would invite preoccupation with Wesley Newcomb Hohfeld, *Fundamental Legal Conceptions*, edited by Walter Wheeler Cook, (New Haven: Yale University Press, 1919), which would invite considering Christopher Columbus Langdell, "Classifications of Rights and Wrongs," *Harvard Law Review* 13(1900): 659, 673.

and preoccupation with race. The more expansive fiduciary obligation began to surface in the post-1965 cases.

As duty of fair representation issues proliferate, we can anticipate that the courts will resort more directly to fiduciary concepts against which to measure union conduct. It is further suggested that the drift of word formula in the last five or six cases examined in this chapter indicates the kind of qualitative evaluation of the union performance of the process and a continuing drift toward standards of reasonable care and other more manageable legal norms.

Finally, I do not anticipate any doctrinal retreat from the principles of *Steele,* although cases like the NLRB's *Handy-Andy*[55] and the Supreme Court's decision in *NAACP v. Federal Power Commission*[56] suggest that the outer limits of governmental action as a constitutional premise with which to control private discrimination have been reached. It is one thing for the Court to decide not to extend further any direct constitutional requirement, such as it did in *NAACP v. FPC;* it would be another, however, to attempt to retreat completely from thirty-three years of judicially evolved doctrine. If my reaction to the current governmental-action direction of the Court is more hopeful optimism than hard-headed analysis, then it is yet another example of the confidence of black people in the principles this country has so long proclaimed but has yet to practice.

---

55. *Supra* footnote 27.
56. 425 U.S. 62, 96 S. Ct. 1806 (1976).

The Conflict between the Duty of Fair Representation and the Limitations on Union Self-Government

Judith P. Vladeck

My point of view is quite different from that of the previous speakers. I am an advocate. I represent unions and am concerned about the duty of fair representation and the increasing obligations imposed on unions to meet this duty.

My question is: How are unions going to provide the service that the duty of fair representation requires? Are the unions going to be able to fulfill the obligations that the courts appear to be imposing upon them? I leave to the scholars the interesting question of how the legal concept of the duty developed — whether it is a constitutional or fiduciary duty, or stems from some other source. I am assuming, however, that as union representatives we accept the responsibility for fairly representing all members in the bargaining unit, whatever the duty's origin.

My primary concern is that while the courts are imposing what appear to be higher and higher standards for the performance of this duty, they do not appear to understand upon whom they are imposing such obligations. There are two essential areas to which I would like to address myself. The first is how the definition of what constitutes the duty of fair representation is to be applied, given the nature of the union as an institution. We should not forget that unions are governed and administered by nonlawyers, working people who come from the shops. The second is that the courts appear not to understand that the union must be strong and secure to be able to provide the kind of service that the courts and the National Labor Relations Board (NLRB) now appear to expect of it.

The invaluable research and editorial assistance of Esta R. Bigler, Esq., are gratefully acknowledged.

I am not as concerned about the first area. At the time of the steel-workers Trilogy,[1] the courts did understand that labor arbitration deals with the law of the shop. As the courts apply the newly developing standards for the performance of the duty of fair representation by unions, they are going to have to accept the fact that the law of the shop on the union's side is administered primarily by laymen.

At the initial but very important stages of the processing of grievances, who is involved on the union side? A worker in the shop. And what makes him capable of interpreting a contract in such a way that it can meet the fiduciary standards imposed by the courts? In some areas where the New York State School of Industrial and Labor Relations holds classes for shop stewards, they learn some of the basic concepts of administration of union contracts. Unfortunately, too few stewards receive this training. It has been our experience in representing blue-collar workers in industrial shops and health care facilities that the level of literacy of the shop steward is often not adequate for making a sharply defined claim. The written grievance statement is frequently incomprehensible and has no clear reference to any specific contractual violation. In this connection, it must be remembered that the shop steward has been chosen by coworkers not because he can read the contract, not because he can effectively present grievances to an employer at the first step, but because they like him.

While the issues of union democracy and fair representation are ones of great concern, and ones often written about, in this context we should consider whether in fact we want to interfere with workers' selection of their shop stewards, or whether they are entitled to have illiterate and ineffective shop stewards. Do we really want to permit unions to designate shop stewards, regardless of the choice of the employees, by the standards of competence in filing grievance reports? Nor are the business agents necessarily much more highly trained. Where do we get business agents? They are smart shop stewards or smart organizers who come up the ladder and become business agents. It is true that lawyers are sometimes used for the actual presentation of the case in arbitration, but often by the time a case is brought to the lawyer, it has gone through two or three stages of the grievance procedure and it is too late to avoid the kinds of problems that the court calls perfunctory or negligent. For example, there are shop stewards and business agents who simply cannot com-prehend the significance of time limits in contracts; they probably have not participated in the negotiations in which the time limits were written into the contract.

---

1. United Steelworkers v. American Mfg. Co., 363 U.S. 564, 46 LRRM 2414 (1960); United Steelworkers v. Warrior & Gulf Navigation Co., 363 U.S. 574, 46 LRRM 2416 (1960); United Steelworkers v. Enterprise Wheel & Car Corp., 363 U.S. 593, 46 LRRM 2423 (1960).

Union lawyers, of course, want to hear the case of the grievant, want to know whether there should be witnesses, want to know whether to subpoena documents, want to know all of these things, but how much time can be spent? Many unions cannot afford to have lawyers present their cases in arbitration. Some unions with the greatest number of grievances are those in marginal industries, where the turnover is greatest, where the economics do not permit the luxury of long hours of preparing a case. The AFL-CIO research department estimated recently that it costs a union $2,200 for a one-day arbitration hearing when it uses the services of an attorney. So that when we talk about the duty of fair representation it seems to me that it would make some sense to consider who is providing the representation: what is the union, what do we expect of unions in providing such representation?

The Necessity for Union Strength

The second area of my concern, which is the more fundamental one, is that while these demands for service to members increase, the NLRB and the courts are quietly, and without any great attention from anyone, cutting away unions' ability to function effectively and to perform the kinds of service that are being demanded of them. I have therefore addressed myself to what I think is a serious flaw in the present demand for fair representation, that is, the present state of the law which makes expansion of the duty an unrealistic requirement. I suggest that we seriously consider the effect of the interference with the internal affairs of unions and the serious damage done to unions in their ability to perform effectively.

In discussing the issue of government interference with union internal affairs we must go back to some elementary questions which seem to trouble the courts. The truth is that neither the courts, nor Congress, for that matter, have ever come to grips with the question of what a union is. Is a union a voluntary organization, with employees free to make their own rules with respect to the acquisition and retention of membership or has the "governmental assistance," that is, certification of unions and the granting of exclusive representation rights, turned it into a quasi-public organization, thus giving the government the right to interfere with internal affairs in the name of public interest? Nor have the courts developed a consistent view of the relationship between the individual and the collective rights of employees in the union as an institution. The courts refuse to acknowledge that the union is only as strong as the commitment of its members, and that the members rely on each other in a social compact to achieve their strength. To the extent that the Board and the courts have interfered with the relationship of unions to their members, the ability of a union to provide the fair representation demanded by the same Board and the courts is undermined.

In this context, I suggest a review of the areas of interference with unions' self-government that are making it unlikely that unions are going to be able to perform the functions being imposed upon them. These areas are the restriction on union discipline, particularly in the cases of strike-breaking and dual unionism; restriction of benefits of super-seniority to shop stewards; interference with unions' elections; and employer financing of members' litigation against the unions as institutions.

Discipline of Strike-Breakers

Perhaps the most dramatic area of such interference is that of the limitation on the right of unions to discipline members who engage in strike-breaking. There is a long list of cases starting with *Allis-Chalmers Manufacturing Co.*[2] in which the Supreme Court made clear that members of the union who cross a picket line may be disciplined and fined. In *Allis-Chalmers* the Court recognized that national labor policy is built on the premise that employees, by pooling their economic strength and acting through a labor organization, have the most effective means for bargaining for improvements in wages. Thus the individual's right to order his relationship with his employer is extinguished while the power vests in the designated representative. That is elaborate language for the simplest and oldest of union concepts: in unity there is strength. In no area of a union's fight for survival is it more important to have such unity than during a strike.

The courts, since *Allis-Chalmers,* have narrowed unions' right to impose discipline on members who break strikes and walk through picket lines. In a series of cases the courts have taken from unions the right to control the retention of membership as well as limiting their power to discipline disloyal members. These cases illustrate the essential hostility of the courts to unions as institutions and the unwillingness to recognize the need of unions to be able, as institutions, to protect themselves against the kind of treachery that in any other organization would not be permitted. In *Scofield*[3] and in a series of cases since, the courts have considered the question of the union's right to impose discipline on a member who resigns from his union during a strike and then engages in strike-breaking. For example, in *Granite State Joint Board*[4] neither the contract nor the union constitution nor by-laws contained any provision concerning the right of a member to resign. However, the union membership had

---

2. 388 U.S. 175, 18 L.Ed. 2d 1123 (1967).
3. 394 U.S. 423, 22 L.Ed. 2d 385 (1969).
4. 409 U.S. 213, 34 L.Ed. 2d 422 (1972).

voted to strike and *voted* that any member aiding or abetting the employer during the strike would be subject to a $2,000 fine. The strike-breaking employees had participated in the strike vote, as well as the strike. The Supreme Court found no limit on resignation, declaring that after resignation the union could not discipline employees. The Court did not understand that a strike vote implies a mutual understanding by the participants that all members will abide by the vote for the duration of the strike and that the guarantee of Section 7 of the National Labor Relations Act (NLRA) of the right to refrain from union activity has been waived by the agreement to strike. The Supreme Court concluded that a union's power over its members is no greater than the union member's contract, and that ends when a member lawfully resigns. If the Supreme Court refused to give force and effect to the members' vote to impose fines on strike-breakers, it certainly would not consider binding a union constitution that prohibited members from strike-breaking. Thus, employees who resigned from the union and engaged in strike-breaking in violation of the union constitution could not be disciplined.[5]

In addition to refusing to honor union proscriptions against strike-breaking, the Board has refused to honor union rules concerning resignation. The facts usually follow the same pattern. Employees resign during a strike and return to work. The resignation does not comply with the union constitution. In one case, the constitution provided that members might resign only within the last ten days of the calendar year, the resignation to be effective sixty days after the end of the calendar year. The Board held that the constitutional provision was too "restrictive" and therefore not a bar to resignation. In addition, the Board found that the imposition of fines on these "resigned employees" also violated the NLRA.[6] In a similar case a union rule providing that sixty days' notice must be given to the union of an intent to resign was found to be violative of the NLRA. Employees were fined for working during a strike after their "resignation," which did not comply with union requirements. The Administrative Law Judge found that, since the employees joined the union pursuant to a union shop clause, they joined under compulsion. Therefore, the judge reasoned, in such a situation all that should be required of members as a condition precedent to resignation is a com-

---

5. Booster Lodge No. 405, IAM (Boeing Co.) v. NLRB, 412 U.S. 84, 36 L.Ed. 2d 764 (1973). The court reasoned that employees have a right under Section 7 of the NLRA to return to work, that is, cease engaging in union activities.

See also, O.K. Tool Co., (Machinists Local 1994), 215 NLRB No. 110; 88 LRRM 1120, in which the union violated the NLRA by enforcing a union constitution that provided in part that resignation from the union did not relieve a member from the obligation to not engage in strike breaking. The Board concluded that the individual's right to refrain from union activity took precedence over the union's right to maintain solidarity during a strike.

6. Master Lock Co. (Auto Workers Local 469) 90 LRRM 1563, 221 NLRB No. 125; General Electric Co. (Auto Workers) 80 LRRM 1411, 197 NLRB No. 93.

mitment to pay dues and fees. Thus "the employee is guaranteed his rights under the Act, while at the same time continuing financial support to the bargaining representative which must represent him."[7] This case illustrates, to my mind, that the NLRB does not understand the social compact among members. How else could it equate loyalty during a strike with a commitment to pay dues and fees?

These cases seem to hold that any limitation on resignation in the union constitution or bylaws will not be given force and effect to bind members. Thus, members have an unlimited right to resign at any time, and by resigning protect themselves from any and all fines or discipline.[8] Thus, although the courts do say that unions retain the right to expel, this becomes meaningless since the unions lose the right to effectively discipline people who engage in what are acts of open disloyalty to their fellow employees and fellow members,[9] and expulsion does not provide a sanction of any weight.

Discipline for Engaging in Dual Unionism

An equally dramatic area is that of interference with the right of unions to discipline members who engage in dual unionism. There is a classic case, *Local Lodge 702, IAM* v. *Loudermilk,*[10] in which the union fined a member for violating a provision of the union constitution that barred dual unionism. The member had supported another union at the premises of another employer, not his own, in a campaign during which another union sought to replace the incumbent. The court found a violation of the free speech provision of the Labor Management Reporting and Disclosure Act (LMRDA), holding in essence that the fine was inappropriate. It reasoned that the union could have taken "defensive action": it could have expelled Mr. Loudermilk or barred him from union meetings, but it could not compel allegiance by the use of a fine, or "nondefensive" action. The court seemed especially concerned that employees not be hampered in their efforts to change bargaining representatives, but it did not consider that Loudermilk's support was for a rival union at another employer's establishment and that his representation was not involved.

A similar case was decided in New York State—*Ballas* v. *McKiernan.*[11] In this case three union members, while continuing to hold union office in their local, supported and campaigned and solicited funds for another

---

7. Ramey Supermarkets (Retail Clerks, Local 322) 226 NLRB No. 20. 28 CCH 752.
8. There is an indication in the cases, however, that if the resignation limitation is part of the collective bargaining agreement such limitation might be valid. Ex-Cell-O Corp., 227 NLRB 87 (1977).
9. Lodge 702, IAM v. Loudermilk, 77 LRRM 2721 (5th Cir. 1971); Degan v. Tugman's & Pilots' Protective Ass'n, 84 LRRM 2569 (N.D. Ohio 1973).
10. 77 LRRM 2721 (5th Cir. 1971).
11. 35 N.Y.2d (1974).

union. When their own union won the election, charges were brought and fines imposed. The New York State court of appeals, after *Loudermilk,* found the fines inappropriate, constituting interference with free speech rights of union members. It should be noted that the employees in question could have resigned from the union, but did not. It seems to me that the court did not understand the importance of presenting a solid front to the employer, or the fact that membership support of a rival erodes union power, making it difficult to fulfill its statutory obligation.

The Super-Seniority Principle
One of the less colorful, but nonetheless significant, areas of the interference with union self-government is that of the Board's restriction on unions in the granting of special privilege through super-seniority to shop stewards. The shop steward plays an important role in contract administration. He is the vital first line in handling grievances, yet his is often a thankless job. In the context of the stringent requirements being imposed by the courts in duty of fair representation cases, it should be remembered that a good shop steward would protect all employees' rights, but it is often difficult for unions to convince members to assume the obligation of shop stewardship and take on the burden of day-to-day grievance handling. As an inducement, they frequently guarantee that the job is for a fixed period of time. One of the few plums that can be offered to a person willing to undertake this responsibility is super-seniority for such things as shift, job classification, or days off. But, the Board in *Dairylea Cooperative, Inc.*[12] found that super-seniority for shop stewards for purposes other than layoff and recall was presumptively unlawful as it encouraged union activity.

In 1977 the broad pronouncement of *Dairylea* seemed to change. The Board found in *McGregor-Werner, Inc.*[13] that super-seniority that permitted lateral bumping to retain a job classification was permissible. In that case, a shop steward, in order to retain his job classification when his shift was eliminated, bumped a more senior employee on the second shift. The Board cited four reasons for finding that super-seniority was permissible. It encouraged the continued presence of a shop steward on the job and on a shift; lateral bumping was the only on-the-job benefit granted; the shop steward was elected; and nonunion employees participated in his election. In *Dairylea,* the shop steward had been appointed by the union and thus the super-seniority was viewed as rewarding a loyal union adherent for having engaged in union activity in the past.

The fact that a shop steward serves as a union agent and an employee at the same time, does cause the NLRB problems, of course, since the

---

12. 219 NLRB 656 (1975) *enf'd,* 531 F.2d 1162 (1976).
13. 227 NLRB 79 (1977).

NLRA forbids the encouragement of union activity. It seems to me, however, that the Board also has trouble understanding that a shop steward is part of the union team and, as such, is subject to its discipline. In *General American Transportation Corp.*[14] the union removed a shop steward from office for failing to conform to union policies: he had filed an unfair labor practice charge instead of utilizing the grievance machinery and then refused to withdraw the charge at the union's request. The Board found the removal to be a coercive interference with the employee's rights; it seems to me that the Board failed to understand that the person involved was an agent of the union and that the union was thus entitled to require him to adhere to its policies.

Election Concerns

Another area of concern is that of elections. Section 401(e) of the LMRDA requires that qualifications for union office be "reasonable."[15] This standard has given the courts a wedge through which to interfere with the requirements unions have set for office. The most recent interpretation of "reasonable" was the Supreme Court's decision that a union rule requiring a candidate for union office to have attended at least half of the union's monthly meetings for a three-year period preceding the election is unreasonable and invalid.[16] The union's arguments that such a rule encourages union attendance and assures more qualified, knowledgeable officers, that members have it in their power to qualify, and that the Secretary of Labor had failed to show that the rule resulted in an undemocratic, entrenched leadership were dismissed by the Court. Rather, the Court viewed the rule as undemocratically excluding 96.5 percent of the membership from holding office and requiring candidates to decide eighteen months in advance that they plan to run for office.

The courts have struck down several union bylaws over the years as unreasonable requirements for office. The Supreme Court in *Wirtz* v. *Hotel, Motel and Club Employees Union, Local 6*,[17] found a bylaw unreasonable which based eligibility on previously holding union office. Specifically, to be a candidate for the position of general officer or district vice-president, a member had to have served in the Assembly, or the Executive Board, or Old Shop Delegates Council. To be eligible for the Executive Board or the Assembly, however, it was only necessary to be a member in good standing for one year. In the Court's view, a limitation that excludes 93 percent of union members from office and gives control to incumbents outweighs the union's concern that because it has a high

---

14. 228 NLRB 102 (1977).
15. 73 Stat. 519 (1959), 29 U.S.C. § 401 (e).
16. Steelworkers Local 3489 v. Usery, 94 LRRM 2203 (1977).
17. 391 U.S. 492, 20 L.Ed. 2d 763 (1968).

turnover, with diverse interests within the local, it is necessary for union officials to gain familiarity with the local's problems by service in lesser offices.

The courts have also struck down as unreasonable a requirement that candidates for office must transfer from a branch local to a parent local, *Hodgson* v. *Local Unions,*[18] and one that a nominee attend all union meetings in the state between the date of his nomination and election, *Hodgson* v. *Operating Engineers.*[19]

The United Electrical Workers had qualifications for office that were designed to ensure equal representation by limiting eligibility to the offices of president and financial secretary-treasurer to employees in one division of the employer, and vice-president and recording secretary to employees in another. These were declared unreasonable in *Hodgson* v. *Electrical Workers.*[20] The union argued that since one division was larger than the other, the only way to prevent all the officers from coming from the larger division was to divide the positions. Thus, all employees' views would be fairly represented since there is no distinction between the positions. The court rejected this view, relying on the fact that the rules prevented members from running for certain offices.

Financing Employee Suits

Of major concern is employers' financing of employee suits against unions. Section 101(a)(4) of the LMRDA provides that no interested employer or employer association shall directly or indirectly finance, encourage, or participate, except as a party, in any action brought pursuant to LMRDA. The purpose was to prevent "interested" employers from taking advantage of the rights accorded union members for their own purposes or weakening unions — causing dissension and unnecessary, expensive litigation. However, the proviso has not prevented employers from trying to finance litigation, sometimes with the blessings of the courts. In *Farowitz* v. *Associated Musicians of Greater New York,*[21] the court found the employer who was financing the employee's suit was not an interested party, notwithstanding its history of suing the union to enjoin it from instructing members to honor picket lines and seeking redress for union members who had been disciplined. The employee plaintiff had been expelled from the union for publishing a bulletin criticizing the union. The employee, with the employer's money, sued the union for reinstatement and damages. Despite this background, the

---

18. 76 LRRM 3025 (6th Cir. 1971).
19. 80 LRRM 3049 (S.D. Miss. 1972).
20. 80 LRRM 2741 (W.D. Pa. 1972).
21. 241 F. Supp. 895, 59 LRRM 2769 (1965).

Court did not find the employer "interested" within the meaning of the statute.

In addition, LMRDA gives unions no protection against employers' financing non-LMRDA litigation. A complaint by the International Brotherhood of Electrical Workers (IBEW) alleging that the employer's financing the employees' defense in a state court suit to collect fines violated Section 101(a)(4) was dismissed for lack of jurisdiction. The court explained that the act confers jurisdiction only over actions against labor unions, not against employers.[22] In that case, the court of appeals stated that employers may not finance the institution of suits by employees, but are free to finance a defense or counterclaim. The court noted that the union had filed charges of interference with internal union affairs under the NLRA, which had been dismissed by the Board. In the Board's view, the offer of legal or financial assistance to strike-breakers is not a violation of the NLRA.[23]

It should also be recalled in this connection that the Board has no restrictions against employers filing charges against unions on behalf of union members. For example, the charges in the *Boeing* case discussed previously had been filed by the employer, not the disciplined employees.

Summary

In reviewing the threats to unions' internal security, it must also be kept in mind that the duty of fair representation is now viewed within the context of the growing effort to expand the use of labor arbitration for litigating rights arising not only from the collective bargaining agreement, but from external law as well — the NLRA, OSHA, ERISA, and Title VII of the Civil Rights Act. We are asking unions, organizations of lay persons, to litigate legal issues that only a few years ago were left to the courts. This is being asked under increasing standards of accountability that unions should not be called upon to meet.

Unions are thus finding themselves to be the victims of countervailing forces — increasing standards of accountability in handling grievances, with an ever-eroding power to enforce discipline and present a united front to employers — all as a result of court and Board decisions. Moreover, the courts are interfering in the internal affairs of unions, from the election of officers to the retention of shop stewards, while allowing employers interested in weakening unions and making them ineffective to finance and institute attacks against them.

---

22. IBEW v. Illinois Bell Telephone Co., 86 LRRM 29588, *aff'd*, 86 LRRM 2580 (CA 7, 1964).
23. Leeds v. Northrop Co., 155 NLRB 1292, 60 LRRM 1482; Standard Plumbing & Heating Co., 185 NLRB 63, 75 LRRM 1065.

I am not suggesting that the development of these two conflicting burdens is a Machiavellian plot on the part of the employers and government to destroy unions, but rather, as I said earlier, evidence of a basic lack of understanding of and sympathy with the nature and purpose of labor organizations.

The Implications of *Hines* v. *Anchor Motor Freight*

Richard Lipsitz

The background essential to understanding the implications of *Hines* v. *Anchor Motor Freight, Inc.*[1] includes a definition of the duty of fair representation, especially as established by the Supreme Court in *Vaca* v. *Sipes.*[2] The Court stated in *Vaca* that Congress, while encouraging employers and unions to establish exclusive grievance and arbitration procedures, did not intend

> to confer upon unions such unlimited discretion to deprive injured employees of all remedies for breach of contract ... *for these reasons, we think the wrongfully discharged employee may bring an action against his employer in the face of a defense based upon the failure to exhaust contractual remedies, provided the employee can prove that the union, as bargaining agent, breached its duty of fair representation in its handling of the employee's grievance.*[3]

Under this definition, however, a defendant labor organization would likely be able to defend itself successfully against a breach of the duty of fair representation motivated by hostility or produced by indifference, if the record supported a fair conclusion that the labor organization had acted in good faith, even if in error. The Supreme Court explained its view in *Vaca:*

> Though we accept the proposition that a union may not arbitrarily ignore a meritorious grievance or process it in a perfunctory fashion, we do not agree that the individual employee has an absolute right to have his grievance taken to arbitration regardless of the provisions of the applicable collective bargaining agreement.[4]

In other words, the Court said that a labor organization must have the contractual power "honestly and in good faith to settle grievances, short of arbitration."

Whether a judge or jury might have arrived at a different conclusion concerning the merits of the grievance was not relevant under the pre-

---

1. Hines v. Anchor Motor Freight Co., 424 U.S. 554 (1976).
2. Vaca v. Sipes, 386 U.S. 171 (1967).
3. Id. (emphasis added).
4. Id.

Hines concept. At that time if the union acted in good faith, even though mistakenly, the duty of fair representation was performed, and a cause of action against the employer would fail under such circumstances.

My view is that in *Hines* the Supreme Court has substantially and radically altered such limitations. *Hines* involved three Anchor Motor Freight employees who were discharged for falsification of expense vouchers presented to the employer after they returned from an over-the-road trucking assignment. A grievance was presented to the first step of the procedure under the Teamsters' collective bargaining agreement with the employer association—a Joint Area Committee (JAC) consisting of an equal number of employer and union representatives. The JAC sustained the discharge and that decision was considered as final and binding as if presented to an arbitrator.[5]

Nevertheless, the plaintiffs insisted that they were guiltless, that the clerk at the motel where the vouchers originated was the culprit who had falsified the records, and that their union should conduct an investigation in order to verify their contentions. The union declined, however, evidently assuring the plaintiffs that they had no need to worry about it.

Once the JAC decision changed the plaintiffs' fears into reality, the *Hines* case was begun in federal court against their employer and the Teamsters. Asserting reliance upon *Vaca,* the employer moved to dismiss on the basis of the conclusion by the JAC that the plaintiffs were discharged for just cause and that such decision was final and binding. The local union asserted the defense that it had represented the employees in good faith and, also, that the JAC decision was final and binding, permitting the union no further recourse to the grievance procedure. In opposition to the defendants' motion for summary judgment, the plaintiffs presented a deposition from the motel clerk admitting that he had falsified the records and that he had pocketed the money the employer had asserted the plaintiffs improperly received. Thus, although the JAC, the employer, and the union had all been unaware of that fact, the plaintiffs had not engaged in any conduct that constituted just cause for their

---

5. Although I am not familiar with any authoritative studies concerning the activities of JACs under the *Hines* or other Teamsters' contracts of a similar character, I know from my own experience of preparing for defense of a duty of fair representation complaint, the JAC may devote five or ten minutes to one case during the course of a meeting in which a number of grievances are heard. At the next level, forty or fifty appeals from the JAC throughout New York State are heard when the State Joint Committee convenes monthly. Although I share the view that labor organizations are being compelled to assume a more and more difficult duty to perform, because of *Hines* and other recent developments, I must assert in all fairness, as a labor union practitioner, that processing of grievances is not the hallmark of labor union accomplishments; there is room for improvement. Collective bargaining agreements are presumably for the benefit of individuals, even though in a group, and in my view, the stricter the standard, the more likely the duty of fair representation will be performed more adequately.

discharges, notwithstanding the final and binding character of the JAC decision.

Federal district court dismissed the complaint against all parties because the JAC decision was final and binding, and because the plaintiffs failed "to show facts comprising bad faith, arbitrariness or perfunctoriness by the union." Upon appeal to the United States court of appeals, the latter affirmed the dismissal against the employer, but reinstated against the union on the grounds there were "sufficient facts from which bad faith or arbitrary conduct could have been found" during a court trial. The plaintiffs filed a writ of certiorari to the United States Supreme Court, seeking review of the dismissal against their employer.[6]

In its decision in *Hines,* the Supreme Court altered and expanded the limits of the duty of fair representation considerably when it held that the employer could not necessarily defend upon a procedure that constituted final and binding arbitration (the unanimous JAC decision):

A union's breach of duty [presumably the failure to fully investigate and/or the negligence involved in not doing so] relieves the employee of an express or implied requirement that disputes be settled through contractual procedures and, if it seriously undermines the integrity of the arbitral process, also removes the bar of the finality provision of the contract.[7]

In another section, the Court summarized its present view of the duty of fair representation:

[Employees] are not entitled to relitigate their discharges merely because they offer newly discovered evidence that the charges against them were false...nevertheless erroneous arbitration decisions cannot stand where an employee's representation by the union has been dishonest, in bad faith, or discriminatory....While the grievance processes...cannot be expected to be error-free, enforcement of the finality provision where the arbitrator has erred is conditioned upon the union's having satisfied its statutory duty fairly to represent the employees in connection with arbitration proceedings....If petitioners prove an erroneous discharge [as in fact had occurred] and respondent union's breach of duty of fair representation tainting the arbitration committee's decision, they are entitled to an appropriate remedy against the employer as well as the union.[8]

Accordingly, under present doctrine, an employer assumes the same risk of liability when it violates an employee's rights, whether by discharge or otherwise, and even though the matter has been resolved either before or as a result of arbitration, where the union itself has failed fully to perform its duty of fair representation. Notwithstanding that an employer, as in *Hines, in good faith* believed it had just cause to discharge the plaintiffs, it is not protected where the union does not perform

---

6. The union accepted the decision, thus requiring it eventually to defend the reinstated complaint.

7. 424 U.S. 554 at 556.

8. Id.

according to required standards, including the obligation to conduct a full investigation of the facts.

Thus, both parties to the collective bargaining agreement stand shoulder to shoulder in a joint responsibility to protect the individual employee against violations of the agreement. Very practically, the employer assumes the risk of being mistaken as to its (perhaps) good-faith belief in the alleged just cause for the action taken, and the union, very clearly, may no longer rely upon its good-faith, but mistaken, belief that the employer was correct and in fact did act upon sufficient grounds. Stated differently, a nonhostile and nondiscriminatory evaluation by the union that the employer would probably be successful at arbitration, because the facts known at the time of the grievance procedure were more supportive of the employer's position than of the employees', no longer constitutes an adequate defense where the union should have conducted a more thorough and complete investigation of the facts with which it would then confront the employer during the grievance procedure.[9]

While from my professional perspective I do not feel too often for the helpless employer, in all fairness I believe *Hines* has expanded the employer obligation. From now on, employers must question more seriously the representations of lower supervision — or for that matter, in a small enterprise the owner's own biases and prejudices must be more carefully regulated — where a potential breach of contract involves employee rights. If an employer is large enough to afford it, I suggest a simple solution — employment of an ombudsman, an impartial person who will, together with the union representative, evaluate an employee grievance objectively, rather than as a management representative.

As to the expanded union obligation, I depart from the good-faith views asserted by some of my colleagues who represent unions; instead I share the view that increasing the standards by which a labor organization is to be judged in the long run will strengthen the democratic fabric which we assert is an outstanding quality of the American labor movement. Assuming *Hines* now requires a higher level of competence, which I believe is clear, especially in regard to investigating and preparing grievances, I suggest several obvious paths for unions to pursue in order to perform adequately. First, training in techniques of investigating and preparing grievances might eliminate errors due to carelessness or lack of

---

9. I am in disagreement with some of my colleagues who believe the contents of footnote 4 to the Supreme Court decision summarizing some of the facts reviewed by the court of appeals (424 U.S. 554) really place *Hines* in the category of cases where union hostility has been demonstrated. While the court sometimes emphasizes a particular view through the technique of using footnotes, the only critical facts in *Hines* are that the employer did not have just cause for the discharges, and that, without regard to the presence or absence of some hostility, where the union through greater prior diligence and less negligence could have brought those post-JAC facts to the JAC, *Hines* would have been decided identically.

diligence. While some cost might be involved, more than likely in such situations, if representatives learn what is expected, such costs would be considerably diminished. The second suggestion requires much more consideration in the decision-making process: if more unions created the kind of Public Review Board that is a feature of the UAW constitution, on the basis of current case law members would be compelled to exhaust that avenue prior to commencing a duty of fair representation lawsuit; and if the Public Review Board is truly independent, as in the UAW, and if it is given adequate authority, it might provide more realistic relief than that which might result from a lawsuit, which in turn should diminish the possibility of expensive lawsuits. To union representatives who are concerned, I suggest that these simple approaches, while not complete answers, will materially reduce membership reliance upon duty of fair representation lawsuits.

Of course, the hostility which too often occurs within a labor organization, especially at the local level when there is political opposition, cannot be corrected by either better training or reliance upon a Public Review Board. *Hines* has expanded the obligation without regard to hostility, however, by requiring more diligent investigation and preparation, a concept which is not likely to damage the interests of the labor movement or its membership.

The Individual Employee's Rights under the Collective Agreement: What Constitutes Fair Representation?

Clyde W. Summers

The Supreme Court's decision in *Vaca* v. *Sipes*[1] is like a giant squid. It has a number of procedural tentacles, any one of which may be more than we can master, but with all of which we must ultimately contend. There is always the danger that we shall be so preoccupied with avoiding the entwining arms that we shall never see the head from which the tentacles grow, and that the whole problem will escape in a cloud of ink. I do not propose now to wrestle the squid or cut through the procedural tentacles; I will leave that to others or to another time. I propose instead to probe only the substantive head and nerve center — the size and shape of the duty of fair representation.

The central substantive proposition of *Vaca* v. *Sipes* can be simply stated: Where the collective agreement gives the union exclusive control over the grievance procedure and arbitration, the individual employee's rights under the collective agreement are limited by the union's duty of fair representation. The employee can sue the employer for breach of his rights under the collective agreement only after first showing that the union has acted unfairly in refusing to process his grievance to arbitration; and he can sue the union for refusing to process his grievance only upon showing that the union acted unfairly. The liabilities of both the employer and the union are dependent on the union's violation of its duty of fair representation.

Although the substantive proposition can be simply stated, its practical content is not easily defined; the term "fair" provides only the starting point, not the ending point, of inquiry. The crucial and difficult question is what standards or guides are to be used in determining whether the

---

1. 386 U.S. 171 (1967).

union's handling of the grievance has been "fair." It is this question which I want to probe.

Roots of the Right to Fair Representation

The right to fair representation had its origin in the cases of *Steele* v. *Louisville & Nashville Railroad,*[2] and *Tunstall* v. *Brotherhood of Locomotive Firemen & Enginemen,*[3] decided in 1944. In those cases, the Supreme Court invalidated seniority clauses negotiated by the union and employer that had the purpose and effect of putting Negroes at the bottom of the seniority list. The Court, in those cases, articulated the basic principle that a union owes a duty to "act fairly" toward and "protect equally" all whom it represents. This duty has two separate tap roots.

First, a union vested with statutory authority as the exclusive representative must have a statutory duty much like that of a governmental body to represent fairly those governed by its agreements. In the words of the Court, the statute imposes on the union in negotiating a collective agreement "at least as exacting a duty to protect equally the members of a craft as the Constitution imposes on a legislature to give equal protection to the interests of those for whom it legislates."[4]

Second, a union that acts as bargaining representative of employees owes to the employees it represents the duty owed by an agent to its principal and by a fiduciary to its beneficiary. In the words of the Court, "It is a principle of general application that the exercise of granted power to act on behalf of others involves the assumption toward them of a duty to exercise the power in their interest and their behalf."[5] The union "chosen to represent a craft must represent all its members, the majority as well as the minority, and it is to act for and not against those whom it represents."[6]

The size and shape of the duty growing from these roots was not described beyond some sketchy outlines colored with value-laden adjectives. In negotiating an agreement, the union need not treat all employees alike, but can make "variations in the contract based on differences relevant to the authorized purposes of the contract," such as seniority, type of work performed, or skill. But, said the Court, the union cannot make "discriminations not based on such relevant differences," and "discriminations based on race alone are obviously irrelevant and invidious."[7]

Later cases have made explicit what was implicit in the roots of the duty. Variations based on differences other than race can be irrelevant

---

2. 323 U.S. 192 (1944).
3. 323 U.S. 210 (1944).
4. 323 U.S. 192 at 202.
5. Id.
6. Id.
7. Id. at 203.

and equally prohibited, and discrimination can be found in different treatment on dismissals, granting of vacations, rates of pay, or manipulation of seniority rights.[8] But the Court has recognized that negotiating agreements requires compromises and adjustments of varied interests and groups. Therefore, "a wide range of reasonableness must be allowed … subject always to complete good faith and honesty of purpose in the exercise of its discretion."[9]

Negotiation versus Administration of Collective Agreements

These are the broad standards to be applied in measuring the individual's right and the union's duty in *negotiating* an agreement. But we are here concerned with the standard to be applied in the *administration* of an agreement after it has been negotiated. The standards are not the same, for the status of the union, the statutory policy, and the practical needs of collective bargaining are quite different in contract administration.

Section 9(a) of the National Labor Relations Act clearly distinguishes between the role of the union in negotiating an agreement and in administering an agreement.[10] Section 9(a) vests the majority union with exclusive authority to negotiate an agreement.[11] But the proviso to Section 9(a) explicitly states that the statute does not give the union exclusive authority in presenting and settling grievances. The statute mandates that the employer must deal exclusively with the union in making an agreement, but the statute expressly permits the employer to adjust grievances with individual employees.[12] The only limitation on the employer in adjusting grievances with the individual employee is that the adjustment

8. See, for example, Wallace Corp. v. NLRB, 323 U.S. 248 (1944); Ford Motor Co. v. Huffman, 345 U.S. 330 (1953); Radio Officers Union v. NLRB, 347 U.S. 17 (1954).
9. Ford Motor Co. v. Huffman, *supra* footnote 8.
10. Section 9(a), in its entirety, states: "Representatives designated or selected for the purposes of collective bargaining by the majority of the employees in a unit appropriate for such purposes, shall be the exclusive representatives of all of the employees in such unit for purposes of collective bargaining with respect to rates of pay, wages, hours of employment, or other conditions of employment: *Provided,* That any individual employee or a group of employees shall have the right at any time to present grievances to their employer and to have them adjusted, without intervention of the bargaining representative, as long as the adjustment is not inconsistent with the terms of a collective bargaining contract or agreement then in effect: *Provided further,* That the bargaining representative has been given opportunity to be present at such adjustment." [49 Stat. 449 (1935)].
11. J. I. Case Co. v. NLRB, 321 U.S. 332 (1944). For a historical study of the majority rule principle in law and practice, see Herbert L. Schreiber, "Origins of Majority Rule and Simultaneous Development of Institutions to Protect the Minority: A Chapter in Early American Labor Law," *Rutgers Law Review* 25 (1971): 237, and Ruth Weyand, "Majority Rule in Collective Bargaining," *Columbia Law Review* 45(1945): 556.
12. Hughes Tool Co. v. NLRB, 147 F.2d 69 (5th Cir. 1945). For the legislative development of the proviso, see Bernard Dunau, "Employee Participation in the Grievance Aspects

not be "inconsistent with the terms" of the collective agreement, and that the union be "given opportunity to be present at such adjustment." Thus, in processing and settling of grievances, the statute gives the union the limited legal status of the right to be present when grievances are adjusted and to insist that adjustments not be inconsistent with the agreement.

Despite the proviso of Section 9(a), unions assert under most collective agreements the exclusive power to process and settle grievances and to carry cases to arbitration.[13] This power of the union to control the grievance procedure, however, does not derive from the statute but from the collective agreement. The union's exclusive control over the administration of the agreement is granted by the employer, not by Congress; the employers have given unions authority by contract that Congress refused to give by statute.

Congress drew a clear line between the negotiation and administration of collective agreements. The explicit judgment of Congress, articulated in Section 9(a), was that the union needed exclusive power to negotiate agreements but not exclusive power to settle grievances arising under the agreements. Indeed, the words of Section 9(a), on their face, indicate a congressional policy that the union should not have exclusive control over grievances, for the words are "any individual employee or a group of employees shall have the *right* at any time to present grievances to their employer and to have them adjusted without the intervention of the bargaining representative."[14]

The fact that unions have, by contract, asserted exclusive control over enforcement of the collective agreement, imposes on them a heavier responsibility to exercise that control on behalf of, rather than against, the individual employee. The collective agreement creates rights in the individual employee that are enforceable under Section 301. In the absence of a union-controlled grievance procedure, the individual can sue and enforce his rights on his behalf.[15] The effect of the contractual provision

---

of Collective Bargaining," *Columbia Law Review* 50 (1950): 751; Clyde W. Summers, "Individual Rights in Collective Agreements and Arbitration," *New York University Law Review* 37 (1972): 362.

13. See David Feller, "General Theory of the Collective Bargaining Agreement," *California Law Review* 61 (1973): 663.

14. Professor Cox has effectively argued that, despite the words used, Congress did not intend that the individual should have a "right" to present grievances, but only that the employer should have a "privilege" to listen. Archibald Cox, "Rights in a Labor Agreement," *Harvard Law Review* 69 (1956): 601. He argued that the individual's right was to fair representation in the grievance procedure, the position adopted by the Court in Vaca v. Sipes.

15. Smith v. Evening News Ass'n, 371 U.S. 195 (1962). The Court in *Vaca* was explicit: "If a grievance and arbitration procedure is included in the contract, but the parties do not intend it to be an exclusive remedy, then a suit for breach of contract will normally be heard even though such procedures have not been exhausted. See Republic Steel Corp. v. Maddox, 379 U.S. 650, 657–658; 6A Corbin, Contracts S1436 (1962)," 386 U.S. 171 at 184, fn. 9.

giving the union exclusive control over the grievance procedure is to deprive the individual of his ability to enforce the contract on his own behalf. The union, having deprived the individual of his ability to enforce his own rights, has a special obligation to act on his behalf.

In practical terms, the union's need for flexibility in negotiating collective agreements is of a different dimension from its need for flexibility in interpreting and applying collective agreements. The collective agreement is a complex package of provisions and benefits. In negotiating an agreement, the union must accommodate the overlapping and competing demands of varied interest groups, surrendering or compromising some demands to achieve others. Relative advantages and disadvantages of different proposals to the various groups must be weighed both singly and in combination. The package put together represents not only a bilateral compromise between the union and the employer, but also a multilateral compromise among interest groups within the union. To negotiate such a package, the union needs, as the Court said in *Ford Motor Co. v. Huffman*,[16] a "wide range of reasonableness."

In contrast, settlement of disputes as to the meaning and application of the collective agreement requires a much narrower range of flexibility. If the meaning of the contract and the facts are clear, then all that is required is to carry out the compromise made when the contract was negotiated. If the contract is ambiguous, then the parties need the flexibility to complete the compromise within the range of reasonable meanings of the agreement. If the facts are unclear, then the parties need no more freedom than to agree on a reasonable determination of the facts.

These differences between contract negotiation and contract administration, reflected in the status of the union, the statutory policy, and the practical needs of the parties, clearly call for different standards for measuring the duty of fair representation. Returning to the roots of the duty, when a union negotiates a contract it is acting like a legislature establishing rules, and like a legislature it is allowed a wide range of reasonableness; but when a union administers a contract it is acting more as an administrative agency enforcing and applying legislation and it must act within the boundaries of established rules. Broader authority and greater discretion are granted to an agent to negotiate a contract than to enforce or apply a contract after it has been made. The duty of fair representation in the administration of the agreement requires enforcement and application or observance and protection of the rights already created by the agreement.

This explanation leads us to search for specific standards for measur-

---

16. 345 U.S. 330 (1952) at 338.

ing the union's duty of fair representation in processing grievances. The search is divided into two major parts: first, a close study of Supreme Court opinions for general guides the Court has provided, and, second, an application of those guides to sample cases which will give them substance and meaning and from which we may draw more specific standards for judging what is fair and unfair in grievance handling. No promise is held out that this will lead us to a comprehensive definition of the duty of fair representation; the most that can be hoped for is that we shall move a step or two along the road toward that goal.

General Guides from the Supreme Court

The only guides provided by the Supreme Court for measuring the union's duty of fair representation in contract administration are those articulated or applied in *Humphrey* v. *Moore*,[17] *Vaca* v. *Sipes*,[18] and *Hines* v. *Anchor Motor Freight*.[19] Although amorphous and incomplete, those guides provide a sense of direction and suggest some inchoate standards to be applied in concrete areas.[20]

In *Humphrey* v. *Moore,* one trucking company absorbed the operation of a second. The local union, which represented employees of both companies, recommended that the two seniority lists be dovetailed; this recommendation was adopted by the Joint Conference Committee. When employees of the first company who were laid off as a result of this dovetailing charged that they had not been fairly represented, the Court, in rejecting this claim, focused on four points. (1) The section of the collective agreement relied upon by the Joint Committee in making its decision "reasonably meant what the Joint Committee said or assumed it meant."[21] (2) The decision to dovetail "was neither unique nor arbitrary," but was a "familiar and equitable solution" in such cases.[22] (3) The local union was free to take a "good faith position...supporting the position of

---

17. 375 U.S. 335 (1964).
18. 386 U.S. 171 (1967).
19. 424 U.S. 554 (1976).
20. Other efforts to develop standards of the duty of fair representation in grievance administration which arrive at results at least partially parallel to the one suggested here include Julia Penny Clark, "The Duty of Fair Representation: A Theoretical Structure," *Texas Law Review* 51 (1973): 119; Feller, "General Theory of the Collective Bargaining Agreement"; Andrew H. Levy, "The Collective Bargaining Agreement as a Limitation on Union Control of Employee Grievances," *University of Pennsylvania Law Review* 118 (1970): 1036; Thomas P. Lewis, "Fair Representation in Grievance Administration: Vaca v. Sipes," *Supreme Court Review* (1967): 81; Paul H. Tobias, "A Plea for the Wrongfully Discharged Employee Abandoned by His Union," *University of Cincinnati Law Review* 41(1972): 55; and "Post-Vaca Standards of the Union's Duty of Fair Representation: Consolidating Bargaining Units," *Villanova Law Review* 19 (1974): 885.
21. 375 U.S. 335 at 345.
22. Id. at 347.

one group of employees against that of another," for it should not "be neutralized when the issue is chiefly between two sets of employees."[23] (4) The disfavored employees were not deprived of a fair hearing, for they had notice of the hearing, and three stewards representing them were present at the hearing and were given every opportunity to state their position. With these four elements present, the union fulfilled its duty of fair representation. Whether something less would have met the minimum standard, we cannot know, but these four elements were considered by the Court as relevant in determining the standard.

In *Vaca* v. *Sipes*,[24] an employee, Owens, who had been on sick leave, was denied reinstatement because of his heart condition. The Court emphasized that the union had pressed the grievance through the grievance procedure, attempted to obtain evidence to support Owens's case, attempted to secure less strenuous work for him, and tried to help him be rehabilitated. Only after all these efforts did the union conclude that arbitration would be fruitless and dismiss the grievance. Beyond holding that this diligence in processing Owens's grievance met the standard of fair representation, the Court by its choice of language and its analysis provided additional guides for the measure of that duty.

The Court in *Vaca* carefully and deliberately selected the terms for describing the duty, and in doing so distinguished between the standards to be used in contract negotiation and administration. Counsel for the union urged that the union's duty should be limited to "acting in complete honesty and good faith," the words used in *Ford Motor Co.* v. *Huffman* to describe the union's duty in negotiating an agreement.[25] The Court, however, rejected these words as an inadequate description of the duty, in effect saying that in the settlement of grievances "complete honesty and good faith" are not enough.

In contrast, the Court defined the duty in broader terms of "wrongfulness"; the individual could sue on the basis of the union's "wrongful refusal to process his grievance."[26] Wrongfulness was elaborated by three principal adjectives used in the alternative—"arbitrary, discriminatory or in bad faith."[27] Repeated emphasis was given to the word "arbitrary," which union counsel had urged the Court not to add to the standard stated in *Ford Motor Co.* v. *Huffman*.[28] Wrongfulness was further elabo-

---

23. Id. at 349.
24. 386 U.S. 171 (1967).
25. David E. Feller, *"Vaca v. Sipes* One Year Later," in *New York University Twenty-first Annual Conference on Labor* (1968), p. 167.
26. 386 U.S. 171 at 185.
27. Id. at 190.
28. *Supra* footnote 16. The courts were slow in recognizing that *Vaca* announced a different standard in processing grievances. See Figueroa de Arroyo v. Sindicato de Trabajadores Packinghouse, AFL-CIO, 425 F.2d 281 (1st Cir. 1970); Jackson v. TWA, Inc., 457 F. 2d 202 (2d Cir. 1972); Dill v. Greyhound Corp., 435 F.2d 231 (6th Cir. 1970).

rated by the Court to include ignoring a meritorious grievance or processing it in a perfunctory manner. Thus, the Court declared, "a union must,
in good faith and in a non-arbitrary manner, make decisions as to the
merits of particular grievances...the union might well have breached its
duty had it ignored Owens' complaint or had it processed it in a perfunctory manner."[29]

These carefully selected terms for describing the duty were more
than elusive adjectives to create a mood; they were used to narrow the
polar positions presented by arguments to the Court and to bring the
standard of fair representation into clearer focus. Rejecting the polar
extremes, the Court emphasized on the one hand that the individual
employee had no "absolute right to have his grievance taken to arbitration, regardless of the provisions of the applicable collective agreement,"[30] for if he could, "the settlement machinery provided by the
contract would be substantially undermined."[31] On the other hand, the
Court emphasized that the union's exclusive control over grievance procedures did not carry with it "unlimited discretion to deprive injured
employees of all remedies for breach of contract."[32]

In narrowing the polar positions of the parties, the Court stated that
the union did not breach its duty "merely because it settled the grievance
short of arbitration,"[33] for in that way "frivolous grievances are ended
prior to the most costly and time-consuming step in the grievance procedures,"[34] and problems of contract interpretation are resolved. But the
union does not fulfill its duty, said the Court, merely by "refraining from
patently wrongful conduct such as racial discrimination or personal hostility."[35] "The union must, in good faith and in a non-arbitrary manner,
make decisions as to the merits of particular grievances."[36]

Proof of violation of the duty of fair representation requires more
than a showing that the evidence supports the individual's claim that he

In 1972, the Court of Appeals of the Fourth Circuit, having read Professor Feller's
article, *supra* footnote 22, pointed out that "repeated references in *Vaca* to 'arbitrary' union
conduct reflected a calculated broadening of the fair representation standard." *Griffin* v.
UAW, 469 F.2d 181, 183 (4th Cir. 1972). Other Courts of Appeals have now explicitly
recognized that the union's duty "to avoid arbitrary conduct" is a distinct and separate
obligation from its duty to treat all factions and segments "without hostility or discrimination," and its duty to exercise its discretion in "complete good faith." See Sanderson v. Ford
Motor Co., 483 F.2d 102 (5th Cir. 1973); Ruzicka v. General Motors Corp., 523 F.2d 306 (6th
Cir. 1975); Kesner v. NLRB, 532 F.2d 1169 (7th Cir. 1975); Beriault v. Local 40, ILWU, 501
F.2d 258 (9th Cir. 1974).

29. 386 U.S. 171 at 194.
30. Id. at 191.
31. Id.
32. Id.
33. Id. at 192.
34. Id. at 191.
35. Id. at 190.
36. Id. at 194.

has been wrongfully discharged;[37] the union's decision that a particular grievance "lacks sufficient merit to justify arbitration" does not become a breach of duty simply "because a judge or jury later found the grievance meritorious."[38] But "a union may not arbitrarily ignore a meritorious grievance or process it in a perfunctory fashion."[39]

In *Hines* v. *Anchor Motor Freight*,[40] a truck driver was discharged for allegedly falsifying a motel receipt, and this discharge was upheld by a Joint Conference Committee. The driver claimed that, had the union adequately investigated, it would have discovered that the falsification was done by the motel clerk, and with this evidence obtained his reinstatement. Although the only issue before the Court was whether the employer could be sued for wrongful discharge when the union had failed to produce evidence at the Joint Conference Committee hearing, the Court restated and extended the standards articulated in *Vaca*. The "duty of fair representation has served as a 'bulwark to prevent arbitrary union conduct against individuals stripped of traditional forms of redress by the provisions of the federal labor law.'"[41] Although the duty does not require "pressing the employee's case to the last step of the grievance process," it does require that a union not "arbitrarily ignore a meritorious grievance or process it in a perfunctory fashion,"[42] for Congress, in putting its blessing on private dispute settlement anticipated that "the contractual machinery would operate within some minimum levels of integrity."[43] If the union fails in its duty in presenting the case at arbitration, the individual employee is not bound by the award. Otherwise, "wrongfully discharged employees would be left without jobs and without a fair opportunity to secure an adequate remedy."[44]

Although the Court's opinions in these three cases do not define the standard of the union's duty of fair representation, they do reject the polar extremes and mark some outer boundaries, thereby providing some guides as to the inner and outer limits of the duty. Those limits are further narrowed, and the standard is given substantive content, by four

---

37. Id. at 193.
38. Id.
39. Id. at 191.
40. 424 U.S. 454 (1976).
41. Id. at 564.
42. Id. at 569.
43. Id. at 571.
44. Id. The Court treated the decision of the Joint Conference Committee as an arbitration award. Because of the bilateral character of the committee and the nature of their operation, their determination should be viewed as a grievance settlement agreed upon by the parties. The characterization of the committee, however, makes no difference in this case, for the union owes at least as much duty to investigate before settling as before arbitrating.

interlacing policies or values which run through all of the Court's opinions from *Humphrey* to *Hines*.

First, the legally enforceable contractual rights that individual employees acquire under collective agreements are valuable personal rights and the union's ability to prevent employees from enforcing those rights should be limited. In the words of the Court in *Vaca*, "We can not believe that Congress in conferring upon employers and unions the power to establish exclusive grievance procedures, intended to confer upon unions unlimited discretion to deprive injured employees of all remedies for breach of contract."[45]

Second, arbitration should not be overburdened with frivolous grievances by allowing an individual employee unilaterally to invoke arbitration or to compel the union to take grievances to arbitration regardless of their merit. The union must be free to sift out wholly frivolous grievances that would only clog the grievance process and must have the power to settle the majority of grievances short of the costlier and more time-consuming steps of arbitration.

Third, the union, as "statutory agent and co-author of the bargaining agreement" should be able to isolate the "major problem areas in the interpretation of the collective bargaining contract"[46] and resolve those problems. Where bargaining has left ambiguities or gaps in the agreement, the union must be able to resolve those ambiguities or fill those gaps by settlement of grievances with the employer.

Fourth, there should be assurance that in settling disputes under collective agreements, "similar complaints will be treated consistently."[47] A problem of interpretation, once settled by the parties in one case, should settle the problem in all other cases. Individual grievants should not be subject to "the vagaries of independent and unsystematic negotiation."[48]

Application of Supreme Court Guides: Seven Sample Cases

The general guides that can be drawn from the Supreme Court opinions are rich in adjectives and illumined by metaphors which articulate values and give a sense of direction. The central core of policies is made explicit, and some of the outer boundaries are marked. But the general guides acquire useful content only when we try to apply them to concrete situations. Only as we confront specific cases and ask ourselves whether the

---

45. 386 U.S. 171 at 186.
46. Id. at 191.
47. Id.
48. Id.

union has fairly represented the grievants can we make the guides more explicit.

Therefore, I would like to examine the application of these guides to seven hypothetical cases and project the results which, it seems to me, the guides require. The hope is that from these results we may discover and articulate more specific standards for measuring whether the union has fulfilled its fiduciary duty to the individual employee in processing and settling his grievance.

The Case of the Paper Promise

The truck drivers of a metropolitan cartage company sue for underpayment of hourly rates, overtime, and vacation pay clearly required by a multiple-employer contract. The drivers had repeatedly complained to the union, but the business agent had refused to take any action. His only excuse was that the employer claimed that he could not afford to pay more.

In this case, by refusing to process grievances the union has effectively set aside a provision of the collective agreement. When the agreement was made, the union had the fullest freedom to negotiate terms that it believed were in the best interests of the employees. That agreement has been ratified by established procedures, and it has created legal rights and duties in the employers as in the union and the employees. Now a union officer has cast aside that negotiation and ratification process as an empty exercise and seeks to treat the contract as consisting of paper promises.

Such a cavalier treatment of the contract is scarcely consistent with the contemplation of the parties, especially for union members who ratified the contract.[49] The expectation of the employees was that they would be paid the rates promised in the contract, not something less which a business agent later deemed adequate. Those expectations are rooted in legal rights. As the Court held in *Smith* v. *Evening News*,[50] the collective agreement created legal rights in the employees that they be paid in accord with its terms. The only thing standing in the way of their legally enforcing those rights is the union's assertion of exclusive control over the procedures for enforcing them and its refusal to use that procedure on the employees' behalf. In *Vaca* the Court said Congress did not

---

49. The processes for union ratification of agreements and settlement of grievances are markedly different in most unions. Ratification is normally by a special process to maximize membership participation, either through referendum vote or approval by a specially selected bargaining committee or representative body. Ratification votes often generate heated debates and large membership turnout, with the recommended agreement being rejected in about 10% of the cases and union negotiators being required to bargain further to obtain different terms. Clyde W. Summers, "Ratification of Collective Agreements," in John T. Dunlop and Neil Chamberlain, *Frontiers of Collective Bargaining* (New York: Harper and Row, 1967), pp. 75–102. This political process of contract ratification contrasts sharply with the essentially administrative process with which grievances are normally handled.

50. 371 U.S. 195 (1962).

intend "to confer upon unions unlimited discretion to deprive employees of all remedies for breach of contract."[51]

Congress has further affirmed that unions should not treat contracts they negotiate so lightly and that employees should be able to rely upon the contract as written. Section 104 of the Landrum-Griffin Act places on unions the duty to provide every employee who so requests a copy of any collective agreement that affects him.[52] The union can scarcely discharge this duty by delivering a document of paper promises that are not to be enforced. The relevance of this section was underlined in *Price* v. *Teamsters:* "Implicit in this provision was the assumption that, absent appropriate amendment of the labor contract, there could be no changes in the Agreement that would abrogate rights contained in it."[53] The purpose of the statute was to enable employees to know their rights under that contract; that purpose is frustrated if they are in fact denied the rights clearly stated in the contract.

None of the policies or values mentioned by the Court weigh against the individual employees' enforcement of their rights under the contract. There is no gap in the contract for the parties to fill or ambiguity for them to resolve by negotiation and settlement in the grievance procedure; the rates of pay are clearly prescribed; the union is not sifting out frivolous grievances, but is ignoring a meritorious grievance. To impose on the union the duty to enforce the employees' rights would not "so overburden the arbitration as to prevent it from functioning successfully,"[54] but would instead require that arbitration successfully perform its function. Indeed, if the union could block enforcement of the employees' rights, in the words of the Court in *Hines,* "The contractual system would then cease to qualify as an adequate mechanism to secure individual redress for damaging failure of the employer to abide by the contract."[55]

There is no practical need for the union's having the power to nullify provisions of the contract by refusing to process grievances. If changed circumstances require changes in the agreement, the union and the employer can, as the court suggested in *Price* v. *Teamsters,*[56] amend the contract. But this should be through affirmative exercise of established procedures for making new contractual rules, not through refusal to use

---

51. 386 U.S. 171 at 186.
52. The words of Section 104 are as follows: "It shall be the duty of the secretary or corresponding principal officer of each labor organization, in the case of a local labor organization, to forward a copy of each collective bargaining agreement made by such labor organization with any employer to any employee whose rights are directly affected by such agreement. ... " [73 Stat. 519 (1959), 29 U.S.C. §§401–531(1970)].
53. 457 F.2d 605 (3rd Cir. 1972) at 610.
54. Vaca v. Sipes, 386 U.S. 171 at 192.
55. 424 U.S. 554 at 571.
56. *Supra* footnote 53.

the procedures for enforcing existing rules. In addition to the right of union members that the union's legislative processes be followed, there are obvious dangers if union officers or grievance committees are allowed to set aside or ignore clear provisions of the collective agreements.

The union's refusal to enforce a clear provision in the collective agreement cuts at the very root of the duty as stated in *Steele*. The union as representative of the employees owes to them the duty an agent owes to his principal. How can an agent, authorized to make a contract on behalf of his principal, make the contract and then deprive his principal of its benefits? The obligation of a union as fiduciary should be to enforce the contract it has made on behalf of the employees it represents. At the very least, the union ought not play "dog in the manger" and assert its control over the grievances so as to bar employees from enforcing the contract in their own behalf. As the Supreme Court said in *Steele*, the duty of the union "is to act for and not against those whom it represents."

The Case of the Painful Principle

The operation of two plants of a national corporation are consolidated into the newer of the two plants. The national agreement covering both plants explicitly provides that when two plants are consolidated in this fashion, seniority shall be governed by length of service with the company. Application of this rule would result in almost all the employees from the older, abandoned plant being in the top third of the combined seniority list and all the layoffs resulting from the consolidation being suffered by the employees in the newer, continuing plant. To avoid this, the local union and management agree to slot the employees according to relative seniority in each plant rather than by straight company seniority. This results in the layoff of some of the employees from the older, abandoned plant. When they file grievances, the local union refuses to process the grievances and the international concurs.

When the union negotiated the national agreement, it had the fullest freedom to negotiate rules governing merger of seniority lists when plants consolidated. The union chose and established by agreement the rule of dovetailing according to company seniority; that agreement has been ratified and is legally binding. The union now seeks to set aside that rule in a particular case and work a result contrary to the contract.

As in the preceding case, the union's refusal to enforce clear provisions in the contract violates its obligation to represent employees who have legal rights under the contract. But in more basic terms, the union's action here is "arbitrary" in the most fundamental meaning of that word —not being governed by rule or principle.[57] The arbitrariness is not in the

---

57. *Black's Law Dictionary* (4th ed. 1957) defines arbitrary as "fixed or done capriciously or at pleasure; without adequate determining principle; ... not governed by any fixed rules or standards."

particular result, removed from its context, for relative seniority would be a rational rule for merging seniority lists. The arbitrariness of the result is that it violates the very rule established to govern it. As was said in *Butler* v. *Teamsters Local 823,* a similar case, "The Local had breached its duty to insist that the employer adhere to the contract and had acquiesced in an irrational interpretation of the contract, thereby discriminating against Butler."[58]

The union's refusal to follow the contractual rule is arbitrary in the same sense that an employer would be arbitrary in discharging an employee for an offense when the posted rule stated a maximum penalty of three months' suspension. It is arbitrary in the same sense that a union would be arbitrary in disqualifying a candidate for union office on grounds neither stated in the constitution nor generally applied. It is arbitrary in the same sense that an administrative agency would be arbitrary in refusing to apply its published rules in a particular case.

If the collective agreement contains no provision on how seniority lists shall be merged when plants are consolidated, the union and employer can fill the gap by agreeing on any result within "the wide range of reasonableness" applicable to negotiating new terms. But when the contract establishes rules, the refusal to follow those rules can only be described as arbitrary. For the union to reject a grievance that correctly protests that the contract is being violated is for it to "arbitrarily ignore a meritorious grievance."

Again, the union can negotiate an amendment to the contract and establish a different rule if experience shows that the existing rule works undesired results. But this should be by procedures appropriate for making contract rules, not by refusing to enforce existing rules in the particular case. The new contract rule should be applicable only prospectively to future consolidations, for to make it effective retroactively to grievances already filed would not only defeat the matured expectations of the employees but would give the change an element of arbitrariness.

The Case of the Settled Ambiguity
Two companies governed by the same multiple-employer contract merge. The contract language is ambiguous, but the consistent practice in similar cases has been to dovetail seniority lists. Union officials, responding to the majority views of the employees involved, agree with the employer that the employees of the smaller, absorbed company should go to the foot of the seniority list. Employees who are laid off — all former employees of the smaller, absorbed company — object, but their grievances are rejected by the union-employer joint committee.

This case is basically no different from the two preceding ones. Although the words of the contract are ambiguous, its meaning has

---

58. 514 F.2d 442 (8th Cir. 1975) at 454.

become settled by past practice. The parties, in the disposition of prior cases, have reached a mutual understanding which is as binding as if it were clearly stated in the printed words. There is no longer an ambiguity, but an established rule. Refusal to follow the established rule in the particular case is arbitrary in the fundamental meaning of the word.

Until the ambiguity is resolved, the parties are free to agree to any interpretation that is within the range of the ambiguity. The court will not substitute its interpretation for that of the parties so long as their interpretation meets the *Humphrey* standard that the contract provision "reasonably meant what the Joint Committee said or assumed it meant."[59] In resolving ambiguities or filling gaps, the parties are completing their contract, not changing it. This can be done through the grievance procedure, for settlement of issues left unresolved or partially resolved during negotiations is one of the major functions of the grievance procedure. Unresolved ambiguities do not create defined contract rights, and employee expectations are not defeated by resolution of ambiguities within the range of reasonable interpretations.

But when the parties have resolved the ambiguity, and by their grievance settlements have established a rule, the policies of *Vaca* come to bear. Among those policies is that "similar complaints will be treated consistently" and that individual grievants not be subject to "the vagaries of independent and unsystematic negotiation."[60] These policies can be fulfilled only if the union follows its own precedents and settles grievances in accordance with established rules.

The fact that in the present case the union responded to majority pressure in endtailing employees from the smaller company does not justify the union's action; it makes it more vulnerable. As the Court said in *Steele,* the union "is to represent all of its members, the majority as well as the minority."[61] The duty to represent equally the interest of the minority limits the legitimizing force of majority rule, for as emphasized by courts of appeal, "It is not proper for a bargaining agent representing all employees to draw distinctions among them based on their political powers within the union."[62] When there is a direct clash of interest between two

---

59. Humphrey v. Moore, 375 U.S. 335 (1964) at 345. The majority of the Court implicitly rejected Justice Goldberg's argument that the parties were free to amend the contract by settlement of a grievance, and that an individual employee could not complain because a grievance settlement was not within the confines of the contract. As was said in *Price* v. *Teamsters,* "The majority adopted the more traditional approach and required the parties to operate within the terms of the contract." The union's action was upheld "only after making a determination that the interpretation involved was reasonable in the light of the contractual language." 457 F.2d 605 at 610.
60. 386 U.S. 171 at 191.
61. 323 U.S. 192 at 202.
62. Ferro v. Railway Express Agency, Inc., 296 F.2d 847 (2d Cir. 1961) at 851 (allegation that union favored politically strong local over politically weak local). Also see O'Mara v.

groups of employees, as in the present case, submission of the issue to majority vote may lead to the conclusion that the decision was not based on legitimate considerations but on political power and was, therefore, arbitrary and discriminatory.[63]

The Case of Grievance Horsetrading

Two discharge cases were pending arbitration. Olsen, who was a fifty-five-year-old warehouse worker and a former union officer, was discharged for intoxication on the job. The evidence against him seemed overwhelming and this was his third offense, but the union committee demanded arbitration because, in their terms, "This is the last thing we can do for Ollie." Schmidt, a truck driver, was discharged for refusing to take out a truck on an assigned load, claiming that the truck was in bad repair and was overloaded. Union investigation had found that the brakes were defective and the load was ten thousand pounds above the legal limits. A week before the scheduled arbitration the company offered to reinstate Olsen if the union would withdraw the Schmidt grievance. The union committee agreed.

This case is but one variation of grievance horsetrading, a practice based on the assumption that the union owns the grievances and is free to trade one grievance for another to gain what it considers a net advantage. The union does not own the grievance, however, for the individual employee acquires legal rights under the collective agreement, and the union is the employee's agent to enforce those rights. In the present case, both Olsen and Schmidt had legal rights not to be discharged without just cause, and the union had a duty to each of them. That duty, under *Vaca*, was, "in a non-arbitrary manner, [to] make decisions as to the merits of particular grievances"[64] and not to ignore meritorious grievances. In this case, the union surrendered Schmidt's right to a job, not because it judged his grievance to be without merit but because it sought a benefit for Olsen. The union did not represent Schmidt's interests, but abandoned them; it acted not for him, but against him.[65] It is difficult to understand how the union in this case could assert with a straight face that it represented Schmidt fairly and equally. To sustain such grievance trading would lead to the result decried in *Hines:* "Wrongfully discharged employees would be left without jobs and without a fair opportunity to secure an adequate remedy."[66]

Erie, Lackawanna R.R., 407 F.2d 674 (2d Cir. 1969); Mount v. International Bhd. of Locomotive Eng'rs, 226 F.2d 604 (6th Cir. 1955).
    63. NLRB v. General Truck Drivers Local 315, 545 F.2d 1173 (9th Cir. 1976); Truck Drivers Local 568 v. NLRB, 379 F.2d 137 (D.C. Cir. 1967).
    64. 386 U.S. 171 at 194.
    65. In Harrison v. United Transportation Union, 530 F.2d 558 (4th Cir. 1975), such trading of discharge grievances was characterized as "arbitrary" and a violation of the duty of fair representation.
    66. 424 U.S. 554 at 571.

A closely related variation of horsetrading was involved in *ILWU, Local 13* v. *Pacific Maritime Association,*[67] where the union accepted the employer's deregistration of a longshoreman in return for the employer granting a grievance concerning the packing of sacks. The rationale of the union was that the trade resulted in the greater good for the greater number because the deregistration involved only one man and sack-packing involved a large number. The response of the court of appeals was blunt: "The deliberate sacrifice of a particular employee as a consideration for other objectives must be a concession the union can not make."[68]

Grievance trading is sometimes done in bulk where a large number of grievances are awaiting arbitration. The employer may agree to grant a number of grievances in return for the union's agreement to withdraw the rest. Among those withdrawn may be grievances of individuals claiming misclassification, layoff out of line of seniority, wrongful denial of promotion, or improper discipline. If the union has evaluated each of the withdrawn grievances and fairly judged that they lack sufficient merit to go to arbitration, then no serious problem of fairness is posed, for the union's action serves the legitimate purpose recognized in *Humphrey* to "sift out wholly frivolous grievances which would only clog the grievance process."[69] This is often not the case, however. The union may not be sifting out wholly frivolous grievances, but rather withdrawing grievances that it believes have merit or that it has not investigated sufficiently to make a judgment.

In analytical terms, such grievance settlements in bulk are the rankest form of arbitrary and discriminatory conduct. The settlement is arbitrary in that the established rules are set aside and the grievances are not decided on their merits but on a wholly unprincipled basis. The grievances are settled because, by happenstance, they are in the backlog when the settlement is made. The settlement is discriminatory in that these particular employees are treated differently from other employees; they are not given equal protection, for the protection of their individual contract rights is abandoned in order to benefit others. The union's fiduciary obligation, at the very least, is to make a good-faith judgment of the merits of the individual's grievance, not to conduct a lottery with his livelihood.

Such bulk settlements may be useful in relieving grievance procedures that have become overburdened at the final steps, but this does not justify wholesale abandonment of employees' rights. Such backlogs do not

---

67. 441 F.2d 1061 (9th Cir. 1971).
68. Id. at 1068.
69. 375 U.S. 335 at 349.

grow overnight but are the result of one or both parties refusing to settle at lower steps of the grievance procedure or to press forward at upper steps. The parties cannot fairly assert exclusive control over procedures to enforce the contract and then shift the burden of their failure properly to use that procedure onto randomly designated employees and make them pay with loss of their job rights. That is an arbitrary and discriminatory imposition on a few employees of the costs of the parties' past failures. The union should not so readily escape its responsibility to aggrieved employees to weigh the merits of the grievances and to seek settlement of those grievances on their merits, nor should the employer so readily escape its liability for breaches of the collective agreement.

The Case of the Unloved Grievant

"Bull Whip Pete" had been promoted to supervisor from the ranks, but after several years he became so abusive and overbearing that he could not work with the men under him. When he was demoted back to the bargaining unit, he bid on a job based on seniority accumulated during the years he worked as a supervisor. The company awarded him the job but when the union protested, the company removed him from the job. The contract language was ambiguous as to accumulation of seniority by supervisors and there were no precedents. The union committee refused to process his grievance with the statement, "He should be ridden out of the plant on a rail."

Two compelling considerations meet here head on. On the one hand, the contract is ambiguous and the parties should be allowed to resolve that ambiguity. At the bargaining table the contract was left incomplete, failing to specify the rule to govern this case; the grievance procedure has provided the parties no prior opportunity to complete their contract. They should now be free to complete it by agreeing to whatever reasonable interpretation best serves their mutual interests and establishing a rule to govern this and future cases. This freedom should be as wide as the ambiguity in the contract, and might well encompass the result reached in this case.

On the other hand, in settling Pete's grievance the union was motivated by personal hostility, which generates arbitrariness and bespeaks bad faith. The union acted against, not for, one whom it was obligated to represent, seeking to destroy rather than to protect his contract rights. In this respect, the case is a paradigm of the failure to represent fairly.[70]

The grievance settlement in this situation cannot claim validity as an act of contract completion, for the parties did not weigh the considerations as to whether a general rule allowing accumulation of seniority during service as a supervisor would serve their mutual interests. Indeed, it is

---

70. See, for example, NLRB v. Local 485, IUE, 454 F.2d 17 (2d Cir. 1972); Miranda Fuel Co., 140 NLRB 181 (1962).

doubtful if they intended to establish a general rule to govern future cases. But if no personal hostility had been involved and they had made a good-faith judgment on the merits, they might well have arrived at the same result. Pete has not necessarily been deprived of any substantive contract right to accumulated seniority; he has clearly been deprived of a procedural right to a fair determination.

There can be no dispute that Pete has been deprived of fair representation and is entitled to legal relief. The problem is to design a remedy that will not unduly impair the parties' freedom to complete the contract by agreeing to a general rule to govern future cases, but which will give Pete a fair determination of his grievance in this particular case. Wrestling with the slippery and entangling problems of remedies is beyond the scope of this paper. It must suffice to say that there is a range of alternatives, one of which is for the court to make the determination, as it can under *Vaca*, with the explicit statement that the court's decision in the particular case shall not be a binding precedent preventing the parties from adopting a different rule in future cases.[71]

The Case of Sudden Statesmanship

Pulaski was discharged for striking a foreman. He claimed that the foreman had provoked him with obscene, abusive language containing ethnic slurs; the foreman claimed that Pulaski started the verbal abuse and shoving match. The union refused to carry the case to arbitration because it believed that there was little chance of winning Pulaski's reinstatement and it did not want to condone fighting. In the past, however, the union had carried every discharge case, including fighting cases, to arbitration, no matter how questionable, and even in some seemingly hopeless cases, the arbitrator had ordered reinstatement without back-pay.

The definition of "discriminate" is to treat unequally; and the union's duty of fair representation, as articulated in *Steele* and subsequent cases, is to "protect equally all those it represents." Here, Pulaski has been discriminated against because he has not been given equal protection by the union; he has been denied access to the arbitration process, which all others similarly situated have enjoyed. He has thereby been denied a chance given to other discharged employees to win a reduced penalty, a chance of substantial value even if it is only a spin on the roulette wheel of arbitration.

The union, of course, cannot be permanently locked into a duty to arbitrate all discharge cases because of its past policy; it must be free to change that policy. But fairness, it seems to me, requires that a change of policy should be made by prospective rule rather than by application in a

---

71. Ordering the parties to reprocess the grievance would only cast the grievant back into the lion's den, and ordering arbitration would give the grievant less than full assurance of fairness if the arbitrator were to be selected by the parties.

particular case that arose before the decision to change was made. Refusing to proceed in the particular case, rather than adopting a prospective rule, not only defeats the expectations of the employee but also presents the risk that the change will not be made in future cases and the purported rule is no rule at all.[72] The standard of fairness suggested here is similar to that imposed on employers in discipline cases — past toleration of violations of even a posted rule may bar discipline until after the employer has given notice that in the future such violations will not be tolerated.

A reverse problem is presented when the union refuses to process a meritorious grievance because the union lacks the resources or decides that the grievance is not worth the cost. Certainly, the union cannot be expected to carry every meritorious grievance to arbitration, for a grievance may be frivolous because of triviality as well as lack of merit.[73] In addition, union members may refuse to assess themselves dues sufficient to arbitrate even substantial grievances. It is one thing, however, for a union to declare an inability or unwillingness to process a meritorious grievance and quite another for the union to bar the individual from processing it on his own behalf. The union's exclusive control over grievances is not one imposed on the union by the statute, but voluntary assumed by the union under the contract.

The union's duty of fair representation would seem to preclude it from preempting enforcement of individuals' rights under the collective agreement when it lacked the ability to perform that function. At least where substantial grievances are involved, fair representation should require the union either to enforce the contract or to allow the individual to enforce the contract on his own behalf.[74]

The Case of the Careless Committeeman
Murphy was discharged for theft of company property. He protested his innocence and, following established practice, filled out a grievance form, signed it, and gave

---

72. The policies which weigh against allowing individuals generally to insist on arbitration do not apply here. No problem of interpretation to be resolved by the parties is involved. The grievance procedure will not be substantially burdened, for there need be only one more case—of the kind the parties have regularly arbitrated in the past. The union is free to adopt for the future a policy of not arbitrating grievances which have little chance of success.

73. The union's decision should appropriately take into account both the value of the grievance to the employee if the arbitration is successful and the likelihood that the arbitrator will be successful. See Sarnelli v. Amalgamated Meat Cutters, Local Union 33, 457 F.2d 807 (6th Cir. 1972); Curth v. Faraday, Inc., 401 F. Supp. 678 (E.D. Mich. 1975).

74. When the individual has a valuable interest at stake, such as in a discharge case, the union could offer to take the case to arbitration on the condition that the employee pay the costs. See Encina v. Tony Lama Boot Co., 448 F.2d 1264 (5th Cir. 1971). The union's failure to do this would seem to raise questions of good faith as to its claim that its refusal to proceed was because the case was not worth the cost. If the employee pays for the arbitration and it is successful, he should be entitled to reimbursement by the union, for he has vindicated his claim that the case was worth the cost.

it to his shop committeeman. The committeeman lost the form and forgot to do anything about it. Murphy assumed that the grievance was being held pending the criminal proceedings. A year later, after he was acquitted by a jury, Murphy discovered that the union had never filed the grievance. He filed a new grievance, which the union carried to arbitration, but the arbitrator dismissed the grievance as not timely.

The duty of fair representation, as stated in *Steele*, is rooted in the basic proposition that the union, in exercising its power to act on behalf of the employee, owes a fiduciary duty to protect the employee's interests. The union, as fiduciary, is entrusted with enforcing the employee's rights under the contract; certainly, it must owe the duty of reasonable care not to default those rights by failing to file the grievance. The union's position in this respect is analogous to that of a lawyer who is retained to enforce a claim, and like a lawyer the union should be liable for negligence that results in loss of that claim. The union can scarcely assert that it has fulfilled the duty to represent fairly when, by its negligence, it has failed to represent at all.

The Court, in *Vaca*, elaborated on the union's duty in grievance handling, saying: "A union can not arbitrarily ignore a meritorious grievance or process it in a perfunctory manner." How can the union meet the standard of processing the grievance in more than a perfunctory manner when it has negligently failed to process it at all? As the court of appeals said in *Ruzicka* v. *General Motors Corp.*, "When a union makes no decision as to the merit of an individual's grievance but merely allows it to expire by failing to take a basic and required step toward resolving it, the union has acted arbitrarily and is liable for a breach of the duty of fair representation."[75]

The union's negligence may take the form of inadequate investigation or presentation of the grievance, leading the union to withdraw a meritorious grievance or lose it in arbitration. For example, in *Minnis* v. *UAW*,[76] an employee was discharged for falsifying a medical form. An alteration was apparent on the face of the form and the union dropped the grievance without investigating the employee's claim that the alteration was made by the doctor's nurse. The union's failure to make this investigation, said the court, was a violation of its duty to represent the employee. Similarly, in *Hines* v. *Anchor Motor Freight*,[77] the local union lost a discharge grievance before the joint area committee because it had failed to investigate the employees' claim that they had not falsified their receipts but that the motel clerk had falsified the motel records.

---

75. 523 F.2d 306 (6th Cir. 1975). For similar cases, see Day v. UAW Local 36, 466 F.2d 181 (4th Cir. 1970); Boone v. Armstrong Cork Co., 384 F.2d 285 (5th Cir. 1967).
76. 531 F.2d 850 (8th Cir. 1975).
77. 424 U.S. 554 (1976).

The union, acting as a fiduciary representing the employees in enforcing their rights under the contract, owes a duty to use reasonable care to investigate the grievance. To settle the grievance, or to present it to arbitration without making reasonable efforts to investigate it, is, in the words of *Vaca*, to "process it in a perfunctory manner."[78]

Requiring a union to use reasonable care in filing, investigating, and processing grievances places a substantial burden on the union. But the burden of reasonable care is borne by every union member who drives a car, every union that owns a union hall, every agent who undertakes a task, and every lawyer who accepts a client. There is no reason why unions should not owe the same duty of reasonable care to those they represent as persons generally owe to strangers.

There are two special reasons why this failure of reasonable care in grievance handling should be considered a violation of the union's duty of fair representation. First, the union has voluntarily assumed, if not aggressively sought, the authority to represent the employees. Having acquired the statutory authority, it has voluntarily expanded that authority by negotiating contractual provisions giving it exclusive control over grievances. It has, thereby, barred the employee from processing his own grievance or suing the employer to enforce his contractual rights. Having commandeered control over the employee's rights under the contract, the union should owe at least the duty to use reasonable care in enforcing those rights. Second, the employer, by giving the union exclusive control over grievances, has insulated himself from the employee's suit unless the union has violated its duty of fair representation. An employer who has wrongfully discharged an employee should not escape liability because of the union's negligence. This would leave the employee who was a victim of two wrongs, one by the union and one by the employer, wholly remediless.

The standard of reasonable care is, of course, a flexible one; it must be shaped to meet the special needs and character of the situation. It should take into account, among other things, the special nature of union organization, the customary practices in grievance handling, the kinds of cases being handled, and the expectations of the employees. But the union, in administering the agreement, must do more than avoid dishonesty, discrimination, arbitrariness, and bad faith. It has voluntarily as-

---

78. In De Arroyo v. Sindicato de Trabajadores Packinghouse, AFL-CIO, 425 F.2d 281 (1st Cir. 1970), the union failed to press the grievances of seven discharged employees because of a good-faith but mistaken belief that they would be reinstated by the NLRB. The court held that this amounted to arbitrary and perfunctory processing of the grievances. In Griffin v. UAW, 469 F.2d 181 (4th Cir. 1972), the union filed its grievance through the management official with whom the grievant had engaged in a fight which led to his discharge. The union's using this channel when another was available was termed "the equivalent of arbitrarily ignoring the grievance or processing it in a perfunctory manner."

sumed the exclusive responsibility and authority to enforce the employees' rights under the contract; its duty of care in representing the employees should be commensurate with that responsibility and authority.

Emerging Principles of Fair Representation

These seven sample cases do not purport to cover the full spectrum of problem situations nor to suggest the multitude of fact variations that arise. They are intended only to provide points of focus for applying the general guides and principles articulated by the Supreme Court to concrete situations. Reflection on these cases, however, does lead us to some more explicit standards for measuring the individual employee's rights under the collective agreement and the union's duty to represent the employee in enforcing the agreement. Six standards seem to emerge quite clearly.

First, the individual employee has a right to have clear and unquestioned terms of the collective agreement which have been made for his benefit followed and enforced until the agreement is properly amended. For the union to refuse to follow or enforce the rules and standards that it has established on behalf of those it represents is arbitrary and constitutes a violation of its fiduciary obligation.

Second, the individual employee has no right to insist on any particular interpretation of an ambiguous provision in a collective agreement, for the union must be free to settle a grievance in accordance with any reasonable interpretation thereof. The individual has a right, however, that ambiguous provisions be applied consistently and that the provision mean the same when applied to him as when applied to other employees. Settlement of similar grievances on different terms is discriminatory and violates the union's duty to represent all employees equally.

Third, the union has no duty to carry every grievance to arbitration, it can sift out grievances that are trivial or lacking in merit. But the individual's right to equal treatment includes equal access to the grievance procedure and arbitration for similar grievances of equal merit.

Fourth, settlement of grievances for improper motives such as personal hostility, political opposition, or racial prejudice constitutes bad faith regardless of the merit of the grievance. The union thereby violates its duty to represent fairly by refusing to process the grievance for these motives even though the employer may not have violated the agreement.

Fifth, the individual employee has a right to have his grievance decided on its own merits. The union violates its duty to represent fairly when it trades an individual's meritorious grievance for the benefit of another individual or of the group. Majority vote does not necessarily validate grievance settlements, but may instead make the settlement suspect as based on political power and not on merit.

Sixth, the union can make good-faith judgments in determining the merits of a grievance, but it owes the employees it represents the duty to use reasonable care and diligence both in investigating grievances in order to make that judgment and in processing and presenting grievances in their behalf.

These standards are obviously not exhaustive, and they lack definitive precision. They do, however, carry us a substantial step beyond the general guides and principles as stated in *Humphrey* v. *Moore, Vaca* v. *Sipes,* and *Hines* v. *Anchor Motor Freight.* They give us a more meaningful understanding of the nature and content of the duty of fair representation and provide more workable guides for deciding concrete cases. Together, they protect the individual's right to representation in grievance handling and, at the same time, allow the union sufficient freedom to fulfill its function in administering the agreement.

The Duty of Fair Representation in Arbitration

Robert J. Rabin

The impact of the duty of fair representation on the conduct of arbitrations and its invitation of greater judicial scrutiny of the arbitration process are important aspects of the problem to explore. It is only by canvassing the whole range of litigation in this area, however, that one can appreciate the institutional implications of the duty of fair representation as it affects unions, employers, and the process of arbitration. Therefore, since other chapters of this volume deal with the big names like *Vaca* v. *Sipes* and *Hines* v. *Anchor Motor Freight, Inc.*, and some of the earlier landmark cases on the duty of fair representation, I will discuss the more obscure cases — those decided at the district or circuit court levels or before the National Labor Relations Board (NLRB).

A systematic reading of the duty of fair representation cases reported in the recent volumes of the LRRM (any other service would do as well) soon produces a sense of déjà vu. With repetition of the names, *Anchor Motor Freight, Kesner,* and *Teamster Local 705,* one soon begins to wonder whether there is but a single case wending its way back and forth between the Board and the courts, or but a handful of recalcitrant employers, careless unions, and disgruntled employees causing all the trouble.

But a careful look at the cases indicates that there is sufficient litigation for all. Many problems arise out of mergers of large trucking concerns; hence a lot of cases involve trucking companies and Teamster locals. And there is a persistent fellow named Kesner, who happens to have a brother who also feels aggrieved, so their names appear in the case tables quite a bit.[1] Those coincidences aside, the volume of duty of fair

Some of the thoughts in this chapter were expressed in an earlier paper written with my colleague Robert F. Koretz, "Arbitration and Individual Rights" published in American Arbitration Association, *The Future of Labor Arbitration in America* (New York: AAA, 1976): 113–57, in conjunction with their Wingspread Conference. I am grateful for the support of the AAA in enabling us to prepare the Wingspread piece and in allowing me to borrow from it. I also wish to thank Syracuse University law student Perry Jacobs for his invaluable research assistance in preparing this paper. Readers who wish a more detailed analysis of the pre-1976 cases may find the Wingspread paper helpful.
1. Anchor Motor Freight was the employer in the landmark Hines decision, referred to later on, in Morton v. Anchor Motor Freight, 90 LRRM 2427 (S.D.N.Y. 1975) as well as in

representation litigation is alarming. A review of six months' worth of LRRM volumes—92 through 94—uncovered no less than thirty-five duty of fair representation cases, or a rate of seventy a year. Who knows how many more lawsuits are settled without a formal court opinion and how many others are resolved by the NLRB without going to a hearing.

The reported cases are but the tip of an iceberg that can have serious institutional repercussions. The concerns expressed by practitioners at the Duty of Fair Representation Conference, at the meeting of the National Academy of Arbitrators in 1977, at a study session conducted by the American Arbitration Association in 1976, and at the Wingspread Conference in 1975 suggest that the duty of fair representation does have a profound impact on the grievance and arbitration process. A part of this impact affects the way in which grievances are handled. Let us hope that greater care is being exercised by unions in processing grievances, for negligent and perfunctory treatment may violate the duty of fair representation in its more modern contours.[2] On the other hand, however, unions may be discouraged from screening out less meritorious grievances for fear of being struck by a duty of fair representation lawsuit.

This latter problem should concern us, for there is an increasing but hard-to-document consensus that close cases are being taken to arbitration more frequently.[3] If so, there is the possibility that a weak grievance

---

Kesner v. NLRB. Aaron Kesner began his litigation after being merged out of a job in 1970. The reader may trace his travail in Teamsters, Local 705, 209 NLRB 46, 86 LRRM 1119 (1974), *rev. denied sub nom* Kesner v. NLRB, 532 F.2d 1169, 92 LRRM 2137 (7th Cir. 1976), *cert. den.* 93 LRRM 2137 and 93 LRRM 3019 (1976). His brother Louis's case — Associated Transport and Local 705, 203 NLRB 139, 83 LRRM 1523 (1973)—is a discrimination rather than a duty of fair representation case.

2. This shift in emphasis from the "arbitrary" and "discriminatory" aspects of the Vaca test to whether the union's conduct was "arbitrary" or "perfunctory" is discussed in Koretz and Rabin, "Arbitration and Individual Rights," 126–29. The shift is best exemplified by such cases as Figueroa de Arroyo v. Sindicato de Trabajadores Packinghouse, 425 F.2d 281, 74 LRRM 2028 (1st Cir. 1970); Griffin v. UAW, 469 F.2d 181, 81 LRRM 2485 (4th Cir. 1972); Ruzicka v. GM, 523 F.2d 306, 90 LRRM 2497 (1975); and Morton v. Anchor Motor Freight, 90 LRRM 2427 (S.D.N.Y. 1975). For decisions in which mere negligent or careless treatment is held not to violate the duty of fair representation, however, see Bazarte v. U.T.U., 429 F.2d 868, 75 LRRM 2017 (3d Cir. 1970) and the NLRB line of cases, such as Teamsters Local 692, 209 NLRB 446, 85 LRRM 1385 (1974), and Operating Engineers Local 18, 144 NLRB 1365, 54 LRRM 1235 (1963).

3. A paper presented by Charles G. Bakaly to the ABA Section on Labor Relations Law reported that according to a University of Michigan survey, 15 percent of all arbitration cases are brought primarily because the union fears a fair representation suit if it drops the grievance. The same survey indicated that management lawyers thought the figure was 23 percent. Report of 1974 Proceedings of ABA Section of Labor Relations Law 102, 105–6 (Chicago: ABA Press, 1975). Several knowledgeable persons recently observed that unions were increasingly taking cases to arbitration because of the threat of *Vaca* lawsuits. Clyde Summers, "The Individual Employee's Rights under the Collective Agreement: What Constitutes Fair Representation," *Proceedings of 27th Annual Meeting of National Academy of Arbitrators*, pp. 14, 32, 36–37, 41, 42, 55 (comments of Lester Asher, Bernard Dunau, and Robert H. Kleeb). Most of the Wingspread participants shared this perception.

will be taken to arbitration but presented inadequately, because the union will see this as preferable to screening out the grievance and defending a duty of fair representation suit. The professional integrity of those who participate in the arbitration process should prevent such a thing from happening, but it does not seem to do so. In the same six-month period just referred to, twelve reported duty of fair representation cases involved challenges to completed arbitration awards—claims, in other words, that the grievance was not handled properly in arbitration. Two dozen such cases in one year indicate a likelihood that unions are sometimes representing grievants inadequately in arbitration.

Even assuming that most of these challenges are without merit, their very existence threatens the arbitration process, first because, as *Hines* teaches, the finality of arbitration awards is jeopardized. More significantly, however, these challenges expose more and more of the arbitration process to review and, because some of the cases are very appealing from the individual's point of view, invite judicial intervention in arbitration.

An Inventory of Problems

Before generalizing about the impact of fair representation on the arbitration process, it would be well to take an inventory of the kinds of problems the courts are picking up. The most serious challenges are found in a couple of cases that have become cause célèbres, but I suggest they are not typical of the grist in the judicial mills these days.

The famous *Hines* case,[4] appears to be an extreme case of perfunctory grievance handling, not likely to arise very often. The discharged drivers, who had an appealing case, were probably victims of the chicanery of the motel clerk and should not have been fired in the first place. Not only did the union fail to pursue certain lines of investigation suggested by the grievants, but it told them that they need not worry and need not hire their own attorney. There was also evidence of union hostility toward these drivers. It is important to stress, however, that the Court in *Hines* did not squarely hold that even these alleged derelictions constituted a breach of the duty of fair representation. It merely held that, assuming the court of appeals was correct in its finding of breach of the duty of fair representation, the resulting arbitration award could be set aside. The court of appeals did not rule on the merits of the grievants' claim either; it held only that they had alleged enough to defeat a union motion for summary judgment. So *Hines* is not only an extreme case, but one that does not focus on the really hard question of how inadequate the

---

4. 424 U.S. 554 (1976).

representation must be before the union's duty is breached. Moreover, while the Court treats the joint committee decision in *Hines* as the equivalent of an award by a neutral arbitrator, I suspect that in reality such decisions are more vulnerable to judicial attack than the traditional arbitrator's award.

Holodnak v. *Avco Corp.*[5] also seems to be a diversion. While Judge Lumbard's trial court decision comes down hard on the perfunctory presentation by the union's lawyer, the second circuit's opinion turns heavily upon Avco's involvement in defense contracts and its conclusion that the First Amendment should have protected the grievant's speech. The appellate court did not focus on the portion of Judge Lumbard's decision condemning the lawyer's performance, nor for that matter did it pay much attention to the lower court's conclusions as to the arbitrator's bias. If, however, the reviewing court meant to endorse Judge Lumbard's findings as to perfunctory lawyering, the case is indeed a significant one. It imposes substantial "procedural" duties on a representative, requiring him at the very least to meet with the grievant in advance, be fully familiar with his case, and allow ample time for preparation. *Holodnak* also questions judgmental and even substantive decisions of the representative, faulting him for taking the perhaps questionable tack of asking for "mercy" for the grievant and for failing to raise and pursue a not-so-obvious claim that the First Amendment controls the case.

Belanger v. *Matteson*[6] is also unique. The union took to arbitration the case of a senior teacher who lost out to a junior for a department head position. The union obviously did a competent job of representing the senior teacher, for it convinced the arbitrator that the qualifications of the two teachers were equal and that under the contract clause the senior teacher was entitled to the position. When Belanger, who then became the aggrieved junior teacher, asked the union to arbitrate his claim, the union understandably balked. It had just won a case for Matteson and did not see how it could try to reverse that case. And even though the employer, in seeking to defend its choice of Belanger, had in effect advocated Belanger's position in Matteson's arbitration, the Supreme Court of Rhode Island held that this was not enough. It decided that by aligning itself with Matteson the union had breached its duty to Belanger. Had the union met with Belanger first, investigated his claim to the job and compared his qualifications with Matteson's, it might properly have taken sides with Matteson. But its right to take a position between two members of the bargaining unit must be "based on a good faith judgment as to the merits

---

5. 381 F. Supp. 191, 87 LRRM 2337 (D. Conn. 1974), *aff'd* in part and *rev'd* in part, 514 F.2d 285, 88 LRRM 2950 (2d Cir. 1975).

6. Belanger v. Matteson, 346 A.2d 124 (R.I. 1975), 91 LRRM 2003, *cert. denied*, 96 Sup. Ct. 1466 (R.I. 1976). The language quoted in the main text is found at 91 LRRM 2007.

of the conflicting claims." Unions will probably now make a genuine effort to investigate the competing claims before espousing one of them to avoid a repeat of *Belanger* v. *Matteson.*

Another well-known case, similar to *Belanger* v. *Matteson,* involves Aaron Kesner, who was squeezed out of a job in a merger of transport companies. The union undertook to press Kesner's claim to seniority rights in the new company, but at arbitration the union in effect said to the panel: We represent Brother Kesner, but he hasn't much of a case. And so the Board, with court approval, held that the union breached its duty of fair representation to Kesner, even though the Board agreed Kesner did not have much of a case and was not in any event entitled to a remedy. The reviewing court put it nicely: "When one's own representative who has been willing to assume that status proclaims a lack of merit, it is indeed likely to be a coup de grace to the claim."[7]

There remains a solid body of law that unions are free to choose in good faith between competing claims within the bargaining unit where there is a legitimate basis for preferring one over the other, but they cannot reach this conclusion without adequate investigation (*Belanger* v. *Matteson*) or lead the unsuspecting grievant to the altar, only to sacrifice him (*Kesner*).[8]

What, then, are the lesser known and more routine cases all about? A typical example is called *Mangiaguerra;*[9] it involves Local 705 of the Teamsters—Aaron Kesner's local. Mr. Mangiaguerra, a truck driver, was fired for refusing an additional assignment upon completion of a run. Drivers were apparently permitted under their contract to refuse subsequent runs if they gave adequate advance notice that they wished to take a layover. The factual issue was whether Mangiaguerra gave this notice. The Joint Board held he did not and sustained the discharge. Mangiaguerra then sued his union for failure to represent him properly. His allegations included: (1) the union representative did not speak to the night dispatcher, who allegedly received Mangiaguerra's call; (2) the union representative was virtually silent at the hearing; (3) the representative failed to point out that Mangiaguerra informed his employer that he was fatigued; (4) the representative did not hold a prior conference with him; (5) the representative failed to object to certain hearsay evidence;

---

7. The Kesner litigation is traced in footnote 1 *supra.* The quoted language is at 92 LRRM 2141.
8. The right to choose between competing interests was made clear in Humphrey v. Moore, 375 U.S. 335 (1964) at 345–49. See also Ford Motor Co. v. Huffman, 345 U.S. 330 (1953) at 338. But limitations have been engrafted upon that right in Belanger, Kesner, and Bieski v. Eastern Automobile Forwarding Co., 396 F.2d 32, 68 LRRM 2411 (3d Cir. 1968).
9. Mangiaguerra v. D & L Transport, Inc., 410 F. Supp. 1022, 92 LRRM 2426 (N.D. Ill. 1976).

and (6) the union was out to get him: he was a member of T.R.U.T.H., an organization critical of the union leadership.

The court found Mangiaguerra's representation adequate. It held that while the union's omissions may have been negligent, no bad faith was shown. It was not enough, said the court, that the representation of the grievant was incompetent or that the union representative was guilty of poor judgment, laxity, or negligence. Furthermore, the court did not find a link between the grievant's political activity and the way his grievance was handled.

An Important Aside

It seems appropriate to pause at this point to consider whether the *Mangiaguerra* court's approach was correct. The cases dealing with the union's obligations in screening cases have shown a gradual shift in focus from the "bad faith" and "discriminatory" aspects of the *Vaca* test to the "arbitrary" and "perfunctory" ingredients of the formula.[10] Indeed, *Vaca* itself involved no claim of union hostility toward Owens, the grievant; the case went further than the earlier duty of fair representation cases involving racial discrimination and added the "arbitrary" and "perfunctory" language. While in *Hines* there was some suggestion of union animosity toward the grievants, the Court relegated that consideration to a footnote; thus it surely did not play an important part in the Court's decision. It appears, then, that in *Hines,* the Court was prepared to find a breach of the duty of fair representation in arbitration even absent a claim of hostility toward the grievant. If this is so, the *Mangiaguerra* court may have given too much weight to the absence of demonstrated bad motive and not enough to the perfunctory performance of the union in arbitration. Of course, even *Hines* does not indicate clearly whether the "perfunctory" test of *Vaca* embraces negligent or careless grievance handling or whether it contemplates conduct more egregious. *Hines* really waffles on this point. On the one hand, the decision indicates that mere error on the union's part does not taint the arbitration and that the employee must show dishonesty, bad faith, or discrimination by the union. Yet the Court ultimately concludes that an arbitration award may be set aside whenever the union breaches its duty of fair representation. Presumably, since the Court in *Hines* repeats the "perfunctory" language of the *Vaca* test, it is prepared to strike down an arbitration award in which the union's presentation is perfunctory. But since, as indicated earlier, the Court assumes for purposes of the appeal that the lower court correctly held that the duty of fair representation was breached, it does not give a direct ruling on how

---

10. See footnote 2, *supra.*

lax the union's performance must be before it is deemed "perfunctory." Perhaps *Mangiaguerra* is simply saying that the union's conduct was not bad enough to overturn the award.

I am not entirely sure that judicial review of completed arbitrations should turn on the same criteria of arbitrary and perfunctory grievance handling as in cases involving the screening out of grievances. When a union decides not to take a case to arbitration, it is weighing an individual's interests against those of the group. Particularly if one accepts the Summers model over the Feller view, and concludes that the individual has a right to take his case to arbitration unless extinguished by an overriding group interest, it is fair to require the union to support on a reasonable basis its decision not to go to arbitration.[11] While a court or board may not be able to substitute its judgment for the union, surely it can require the union to apply rational standards in making this decision. Under this view a perfunctory or arbitrary decision will not stand because it cannot be said to serve a legitimate group interest.

But when the case actually goes to arbitration, the union has then aligned itself with the individual. It is no longer appropriate to require the union to justify its stance on the basis of a rational, careful decision to oppose the individual's position in the name of a larger group interest. There is no longer a need to confine the union's discretion by striking down decisions that are arbitrary or perfunctory, for when the union takes the case to arbitration, the individual is getting exactly the same services as anyone else. To the extent those services are inadequate, the problem is a political one, to be remedied by pressures on the bargaining agent rather than through the judicial process. To allow a court to overturn an arbitration award on a mere showing of perfunctory or arbitrary performance, where no hostility to the grievant is shown, is a broad invitation for judicial review. It gives courts a degree of oversight not otherwise tolerated when an arbitration award is challenged on grounds other than duty of fair representation and jeopardizes the finality of arbitration awards. Of course, if arbitrary and perfunctory treatment is evidence of hostility toward the grievant, it is an appropriate matter for judicial review.

When the courts do step in, they understandably seem to find the terrain uncomfortable. Second-guessing a union's decision not to take a case to arbitration is hard enough; assessing its tactics and trial techniques

---

11. Professor Summers's view is expressed in his article in this volume. Professor Feller's position is set forth in a monumental article: David Feller, "A General Theory of the Collective Bargaining Agreement," *California Law Review* 61 (1973): 663. Any attempt to summarize their arguments would be inadequate. Their positions polarize as to the extent to which the individual has the right to control his grievance.

may well be impossible, let alone inappropriate.[12] Perhaps that is why the courts, except in the egregious cases (mostly the "name" cases already mentioned), seldom disturb arbitration awards in the name of fair representation. This may suggest, at any rate, that judicial review is not an adequate device for ensuring fair representation in arbitration.

All of this means that the responsibility for seeing that the individual does not get a raw deal in arbitration, as seems to have been Mr. Mangiaguerra's plight, belongs in the first instance to those involved in the arbitration process. Failure to police the arbitration process internally will surely result in judicial intervention.

Additional Problems

Most cases in which courts have reviewed completed arbitrations deal with claims involving bad judgment at worst. Of course one can never be certain from a judicial opinion written in defense of the result just reached how egregious the union's conduct was. A sampling of typical cases indicates that, for the most part, they involve contentions such as failure to inform the grievant that his case would be heard; failure to produce readily available medical evidence; allowing the company's representative to closet himself with the arbitrator; general lack of preparation; failure to interview certain people; failure to cross-examine; and failure to warn the grievant of consequences of refusing to take a sobriety test.[13] The courts seldom disturb the original result in these cases, and to the extent that these cases involve reasonable judgments about trial tac-

---

12. The best example I have found of the inappropriateness of judicial review in these settings is Easley v. Allied & Technical Workers, 377 F. Supp. 729, 87 LRRM 2295 (M.D. Ala. 1974), *aff'd* 524 F.2d 1230, 91 LRRM 2512 (5th Cir. 1975). This case is a painstaking review of the tactics used by a respected labor attorney, which concludes, properly, I think, that the individual was adequately represented.

13. See, for example, Siskey v. Teamsters Local 261, 419 F. Supp. 48, 93 LRRM 2200 (1976) (failure to inform grievant that his grievance would be presented and failure to discover and introduce a medical report do not violate the duty of fair representation; no evidence that grievant's case was prejudiced by these omissions); Hardee v. Allstate Services, Inc., 537 F.2d 1255, 92 LRRM 3342 (4th Cir. 1976) (allegation of general lack of preparation and effort not enough to make out a duty of fair representation claim; some evidence to suggest grievance was fully and vigorously presented, particularly where grievant congratulated union representative on his performance); Marietta v. Cities Service Oil Co., 414 F. Supp. 1029, 92 LRRM 2867 (D.N.J. 1976) (allegations of failure to consult employee at each stage of grievance procedure and of bad faith and conspiracy do not raise triable issue; allegation of failure to gather supporting evidence does raise triable issue); Cannon v. Consolidated Freightways, 524 F.2d 290, 90 LRRM 2996 (7th Cir. 1975) (no breach of duty of fair representation in failure to challenge propriety of "sobriety" test promulgated by employer; evidence shows grievant was aware of consequences of refusal to submit to test); Ogelsby v. Terminal Transport Co., 543 F.2d 1117, 94 LRRM 2252 (5th Cir. 1976) (union would breach duty of fair representation where it allows employer's representative to remain in room with arbitrator; but summary judgment granted where petition fails to allege sufficient facts).

tics, the courts should leave them alone. To the extent they involve egregious omissions such as failure to interview witnesses or pursue obvious lines of inquiry, however, objective judicial review is possible and courts should not hesitate to intervene.

The union's handling of some cases may have fallen below a tolerable level, with no effective judicial intervention. In one split decision, for example, the NLRB allowed an arbitration award to stand where evidence came before the arbitrator that the business agent opposed taking the grievance to arbitration. The union may well have faced a conflict of interest in that case.[14]

In sum, however, the postarbitration fair representation cases do not yet raise specific threats to the integrity of arbitration, nor do they reveal egregious breaches of the union's duty of fair representation. Most of the problems they uncover are procedural, such as failing to listen to the individual, to follow up lines of investigation suggested by him, to observe time limits, or to avoid conflicts of interest. These omissions are inexcusable and obvious enough that unions should be able to correct them. With the possible exception of *Holodnak*, though, courts are not second-guessing the trial tactics of union representatives or their choices of substantive theories of the case.

Yet the flood of litigation remains, and this has undesirable effects. It jeopardizes finality and diverts energies from the union's task of effectively representing its constituency by pressing legitimate arbitration cases. More significantly, as courts look more closely at the arbitration process, which these cases demand they do, they will inevitably have things to say about arbitration. In New York State, the *Susquehanna Valley* line of cases,[15] which gives courts the right to circumscribe arbitration in

---

14. Teamsters, Local 542 (Golden Hill Convalescent Hospital), 223 NLRB No. 72, 91 LRRM 1556 (1976). Similarly "close" cases include Steinman v. Spector Freight, 476 F.2d 437, 83 LRRM 2285 (2d Cir. 1973) (see also earlier litigation cited in opinion; NLRB had earlier found that union's representation was languid and perfunctory); Provenzino v. Merchants Forwarding, 363 F. Supp. 168, 84 LRRM 2212 (E.D. Mich. 1973) (individuals who had engaged in dissident activity within union alleged that union's presentation to Joint Committee was restrained or neutral); Dente v. Masters, Mates & Pilots, 429 F.2d 10, 84 LRRM 2982 (9th Cir. 1974) (union's negligence in delaying case is not actionable even where arbitrator reduces the back-pay award on that account); Walden v. Teamsters, 468 F.2d 196, 81 LRRM 2608 (4th Cir. 1972) (individual asserts that union should have consulted a lawyer and should have objected to certain lines of evidence); Heltsey v. UMW, 78 LRRM 2633 (Ct. App. Ky. 1971) (individual discharged for participation in wildcat strike; umpire had received political contributions from union); Easley v. Allied Workers 377 F. Supp. 729, 87 LRRM 2295 (M.D. Ala. 1974) (union lawyer, whom individuals asked to represent them, alleged to have conflict of interest where the grievants are charged with leading wildcat strike, since excuse of individuals would tend to implicate union).

15. Central School Dist. v. Susquehanna Valley Teachers Ass'n, 37 N.Y. 2d 614, 339 N.E.2d 132, 376 N.Y.S.2d 427 (1975); Union Free School District v. Nyquist, 38 N.Y.2d 137, 341 N.E.2d 532, 379 N.Y.S.2d 10 (1975). For a discussion of these cases see Robert F. Koretz and Robert J. Rabin, "Labor Relations Law," *Syracuse Law Review* 28 (1977): 75, 91–98.

the name of public policy, seems to reflect some judicial uneasiness about the competence of arbitration to deal with certain issues. The *Antinore*[16] decision, while upholding the use of arbitration to resolve claims once handled through civil service, treats arbitration as a second-class form of adjudication, a sleazy sort of frontier justice at best. And as arbitrators deal increasingly with public rights, judicial intervention will rise. All of this is accelerated when individuals ask courts to review completed arbitration awards. Still more may be at stake if courts permit the awarding of counsel fees in duty of fair representation cases, a course strongly suggested in recent cases.[17]

Some Solutions

The abuses challenged in the cases discussed ought to be corrected within the arbitration process itself; if they are not, judicial intervention will be both inevitable and necessary. Yet, judicial review of completed awards is a poor solution: it is clumsy and difficult. It may undo arbitration awards that really should stand, and it may fail to catch cases in which relief for the individual is warranted. I would like to suggest, instead, some modest steps for self-reform.

First-line responsibility should rest with arbitrators themselves. Arbitrators should ensure that all aspects of the case are adequately explored, particularly where they suspect that the union is not doing an adequate job — deliberately or otherwise. Most arbitrators who have discussed this point agree that arbitrators may take an active role, if only to develop a full record on which to base a reasoned decision. There are, however, pockets of resistance to their taking too active a role. The parties bring the case, so the argument runs, and they and not the arbitrators ought to control the lines of questioning that are pursued.[18]

There should be some modification of this position. In reading the postarbitration cases, one finds that it is extremely difficult to overturn a completed award in the name of a breach of the duty of fair representation. A well-reasoned and well-written arbitration award may convince the court that justice was done. The arbitrator is the last neutral body in a position to properly assess whether the individual has had his day in court, and he ought to make sure the individual's case has been adequately developed.

---

16. Antinore v. State of New York, 49 A.D.2d 6, 371 N.Y.S.2d 213 (4th Dept. 1975), *aff'd,* 40 N.Y.2d 921, 358 N.E.2d 268, 389 N.Y.S.2d 576 (1976).

17. See, for example, Scott v. Teamsters Local 377, 496 F.2d 276, (6th Cir. 1977), 94 LRRM 2505.

18. This point was discussed in the commentary following Professor Summers's 1974 presentation to the National Academy of Arbitrators, cited in note 3 *supra,* at pp. 46 and 57.

The recently promulgated Code of Professional Responsibility for Arbitrators does not, in my judgment, make sufficiently clear the arbitrator's role in such cases.[19] In dealing with "consent awards," for example, the code directs the arbitrator to see to it that the award is "proper, fair, sound and lawful" before adopting it. This requires some activism on his part, as the accompanying code amplifying statement provides:

Before complying with such a request [for a consent award] an arbitrator must be certain that he or she understands the suggested settlement adequately in order to appraise its terms. If it appears that pertinent facts or circumstances may not have been disclosed, the arbitrator *should take the initiative* to assure that all significant aspects of the case are fully understood. To this end, the arbitrator *may request additional specific information* and may question witnesses at a hearing.

This obligation should be elevated to a general code provision, applicable not just to consent awards but to the entire conduct of the hearing. This approach is hinted at in an "illustrative" or "explanatory" comment to the code:

An arbitrator may ... question the parties' representatives or witnesses, when necessary or advisable, to obtain additional or pertinent information; and request that the parties submit additional evidence, either at the hearing or by subsequent filing.

It deserves to be made an outright and clear code provision.

In cases where the union is faced with a conflict of interest, it may be wise to allow the individual to present his own case with the assistance of outside counsel. Such a situation could arise, for example, where the company discharges the leader of a wildcat strike which the union tried to prevent. The union could drop out altogether, leaving the conduct of the case to the individual, or some sort of tripartite proceeding could be arranged.

Tripartite proceedings can become three-ring circuses, as a recent decision, *Hotel Employees* v. *Michaelson's*, illustrates. The individual showed up with his own lawyer, and the arbitrator had to develop a procedure that would bind both of the parties to the agreement and provide a result that would be final for the individual. The court, for the most part, endorsed his interim award setting up such a procedure.[20]

The tripartite arrangement probably cannot be imposed upon the parties, however, because they alone control the arbitration machinery; therefore, if they object to third-party intervention, the arbitrator may be powerless to require it. The parties may have good reason to oppose such

---

19. Code of Professional Responsibility for Arbitrators of Labor-Management Disputes of the National Academy of Arbitrators, American Arbitration Association and Federal Mediation and Conciliation Service (1974). The sections quoted in the text are found, respectively, at pages 12 and 19 of the code (emphasis added).

20. Hotel Employees v. Michaelson's Food Service, 545 F.2d 1248 (9th Cir. 1976), 94 LRRM 2014. The arbitrator's interim award may be found at 61 LA 1195 (1973).

intervention, for the individual may pitch his case on grounds that, while best for his case, jeopardize some larger principle in the long run. On the other hand, this concern may be outweighed by the virtual certainty that a court will not overturn an arbitration in which the individual is given a full opportunity to develop his own case.

An alternative model would be for the union to sit down with the individual and his counsel and consider all the approaches and evidence urged by them. The union might develop a correspondence file in which it responds to all suggestions made by the grievant. The grievant's counsel would be allowed to attend the hearing and call for recesses to discuss matters with the union, but would not be given the right of direct participation. This approach would minimize the chance of missing lines of investigation urged by the grievants. If the union deals honestly and openly with the individual, few grounds for challenge would remain.

Various institutional safeguards within the union should also be considered. Like the work of the UAW Public Review Board, a union might provide an independent ombudsman who would represent in arbitration those individuals who felt the union's interests were not aligned with their own.

Serious attention should be given to the creation of a code of professional responsibility for representatives who present cases in arbitration. I like to think that when a union assigns a lawyer to a case that it would rather not take to arbitration, that lawyer's sense of professional responsibility will ensure that he does the best possible job for the individual. Cynics will of course disagree. But there is no body of rules that now tells a business agent or management personnel director, for that matter, of expected norms in arbitration. Setting out minimal standards of representation would be a first step in instilling a sense of professional obligation in those who present cases in arbitration.

These standards, which should be developed by practitioners who regularly participate in arbitrations, could include minimal standards for meeting with the aggrieved, requesting his suggestions for how to proceed and what evidence to marshall, notifying him of the hearing, consulting him regularly at the hearing, and so forth. There should be a requirement of full disclosure of any possible conflict or incongruity of interest between the individual and his union. In such a case the individual should be advised of his right to seek outside counsel to advise the union as to the disposition of the case. The individual who agreed to let the union proceed alone in the face of such a disclosure would be in a far less favorable position later to claim a breach of the union's duty.

Where potential duty of fair representation problems are perceived in arbitration, it might well serve the interests of all concerned to make a transcript. It is hard enough for a court to review an arbitration proceeding. If the arbitration is conducted fairly, a court can readily be convinced of this by an examination of the transcript. Absence of a transcript, on the other hand, may add to the court's distaste for the arbitration process.

There is a need to develop a segment of the bar skilled in representing individuals who come in conflict with their unions. Were such practitioners available on a regular basis, the parties might be more willing to allow them to participate in a tripartite proceeding. Such lawyers could do an effective job of screening out frivolous complaints and convincing the union to do something about grievances that are real. Most of the skilled labor practitioners work for unions or management; they are reluctant to appear in a role that will jeopardize their relationship with client or adversary. Perhaps some of these taboos should come down, and management and union lawyers should recognize the need to represent individual grievants. In the long run this would be beneficial for all interests.

Enforcement of the Right to Fair Representation: Alternative Forums

David Y. Klein

Labor arbitration is an alternative to an action for breach of contract under the Labor Management Relations Act (LMRA). It is the search for a similar alternative in the area of the duty of fair representation that requires attention today. The primary current method of redress available to union members who believe that their right to fair representation has been breached by their bargaining representative is a public review board. At the present time, however, there are only two so-called public review boards operating as final appellate tribunals within the union system of internal remedies in the United States—one of these serves the Western Association of Pulp and Paper Workers, the other, the United Auto Workers (UAW). In addition, the American Federation of Teachers provides for arbitration of certain types of disputes between the federation and its members in a system that employs neutrals and therefore might be considered a form of public review board.

Public review boards, as they are constituted today, do not actually qualify as alternative forums, at least in the area of duty of fair representation, but with certain changes, particularly if the institution were to become a general part of the labor union scene instead of an isolated example as is now the case, it would be readily accepted by the courts as an alternative remedial forum. The courts would then defer to them much as they do in the case of the labor arbitrator.

An action for breach of the duty of fair representation generally sounds in tort, although a few jurisdictions recognize it as contractual as well. In any case, it is virtually universally true that a member who would sue his union for breach of its fiduciary responsibility of fair representation must first exhaust whatever internal remedies are provided him under his union's constitution. Most unions provide some form of internal remedies, but many limit their internal appellate processes to issues arising out of internal disciplinary proceedings.[1] I am not aware of any

---

1. Cf., e.g., Lucas v. Philco Ford Co., 380 F. Supp. 139 (D.C.E.D. Pa., 1973). The argument that IAM Constitution providing for fine of offending member and that fine

union that expressly provides in its constitution that a member may seek redress within the internal remedies procedures for a breach of the duty of fair representation. Furthermore, the procedural remedies vary widely from union to union, but for those that do provide some internal remedy this procedure usually culminates in appeal to the constitutional convention of the union, which meets at multiyear intervals. A few unions, however, have attempted to provide a more effective system of remedies.

The UAW has adopted a system of internal remedies that involves essentially a three-step procedure culminating in an appeal to a public review board. The board, comprised of seven persons who are not members of the union or otherwise associated with it, has been given— concurrently with the union's Convention Appeals Committee—ultimate appellate jurisdiction within the union. The member is required first to initiate his claim with his local union membership. If it is denied, he may take an appeal to the International Executive Board. Finally, if he has not been able to achieve the desired remedy, he may appeal to the Public Review Board (PRB) or, alternatively, to a Constitutional Convention Appeals Committee, which is comprised of a member selected by lot from among delegates to each constitutional convention for two-year terms. The appeals committee meets semiannually. The procedure is designed to be essentially cost free and to provide a final adjudication of a claim within a period of approximately nine months to a year. The unique aspect of the procedure is, of course, the Public Review Board, which the union has established as an independent tribunal with the notion that— comprised as it is by "outsiders"—its decisions could not be the result of political considerations, as might be the case in a forum comprised of members of the organization. The decisions of the PRB are final and binding on both the member and the union. The board has a professional staff to assist it and control over its own budget and bank accounts, which the union is obliged to replenish quarterly.

The board was created in 1957, and has been in existence since that time. It has cost the union over one million dollars in operational expenses thus far, which works out to an average annual cost per member of somewhere in the neighborhood of five cents. It has also reversed decisions made by the local unions and the International Executive Board a considerable number of times, some of which have been acutely painful to the union's leadership.

---

could be made payable to aggrieved member asserting a breach of duty of fair representation claim was rejected by court which held the remedy "inadequate," therefore excusing the member from the requirement that he exhaust his internal remedies.

An Effective Alternative Forum

Such an institution, I submit, has the essential ingredients to constitute an effective alternative forum for a member who wishes to assert a claim of breach of duty of fair representation. Indeed, in every such case in which the union is involved in a judicial forum, UAW attorneys uniformly make this assertion in support of a motion to dismiss the proceedings when the member has not exhausted his internal remedies. The union's record of success in asserting this claim has been high.[2]

Nevertheless, there are some chinks which are beginning to appear in the armor of the union in respect to the willingness of the courts to defer to its internal remedies procedures. These breaches will continue to widen, however, because the power of the Public Review Board to act in cases sounding in the nature of a breach of the duty of fair representation is tied to a bad-faith standard, whereas courts are now talking in terms of arbitrary, perfunctory, and even negligent processing of grievances.[3] Currently, in order to assert a claim over the processing of a grievance before the Public Review Board, the member must assert that his grievance was mishandled by reason of "fraud, discrimination or collusion with management."[4]

The UAW acknowledges that it has a duty of fair representation to its members. Moreover, it acknowledges that its members may assert a claim for a breach of the duty of fair representation within the system of internal remedies. It does not concede to its members, however, that arbitrary, perfunctory, or negligent conduct amounts to a breach of the duty of fair representation, nor does it permit them even to assert this type of claim before the PRB, since the standard of review is jurisdictional. That is, unless the requisite claim is made (fraud, discrimination, or collusion) the board may not entertain it.

Members of the union are turning increasingly to the civil courts to seek relief for alleged breach of the duty of fair representation. In 1976 alone I was called upon to file affidavits of nonexhaustion in twenty-four cases, as opposed to sixteen in 1975 and sixteen in 1974. In each of these cases where the member has not exhausted the internal remedies, the union has filed a motion for summary judgment on this basis, and it has enjoyed great success in this respect. Two recent cases, however, suggest a cause for concern.

---

2. Sedlarik v. General Motors Corp., 78 LRRM 2232; McCloskey v. General Motors Corp., 78 LRRM 2371.
3. Vaca v. Sipes, 386 U.S. 171 (1967); Amalgamated Ass'n. of Motor Coach Employees v. Lockridge, 403 U.S. 274 (1971); Ruzicka v. General Motors, 523 F.2d 306 (6th Cir. 1975).
4. Constitution International Union, UAW (1974), Article 33, § 8(b).

The Ruzicka Case

The first of these cases is *Ruzicka* v. *General Motors Corp.*[5] Mr. Ruzicka was discharged by General Motors (GM) in 1970 for allegedly being intoxicated on the job and using threatening and abusive language toward his superiors. He grieved. The grievance was processed to the third step of the procedure; to invoke arbitration, the union was required by the contract to file a statement of unadjusted grievance simultaneously with GM. Ruzicka's local allegedly never filed such a statement (this claim is disputed) although it had sought and received two time extensions to do so. Once the due date for the statement had passed, GM had no further obligation to arbitrate it under the national agreement, and, when presented with a subsequent demand that it do so, it declined. When Ruzicka learned what had happened, he filed charges against the chairman of his shop committee, claiming that he had willfully failed to perform his official responsibility by failing to file the required statement. The charges went to trial. The trial committee concluded that the committeeman had been negligent, but not guilty of willful inaction. This decision was appealed to the Public Review Board, which affirmed it. It should be noted that had Ruzicka prevailed, this would not have affected the nonarbitration of his grievance: charges are designed to penalize a wrongdoer but not to effect the remedy of the substantive injury sustained.

Ruzicka, in the meantime, also instituted a claim against his local for wrongful processing of his grievance. This claim was rejected by his membership. Ruzicka appealed, but processing of the appeal was delayed while local union officials attempted to file a "policy grievance," to require General Motors to consider Ruzicka's grievance despite the procedural defect. The policy grievance failed, however. At this point Ruzicka abandoned his efforts to secure an internal remedy and filed a complaint in federal court against both GM and the UAW. The district court dismissed the case, concluding that there was no unfair representation because Ruzicka's committeeman had merely neglected to file the required statement. The court found that the plaintiff had failed to show that hostility had tainted the committeeman's conduct.

The U.S. Court of Appeals for the Sixth Circuit reversed the district court. As an interesting aside, one of the panel members assigned to the case was Wade McCree, now solicitor general and a former member of the Public Review Board. The court said that union action that is arbitrary or discriminatory need not be motivated by bad faith to amount to unfair representation. It continued:

Having sought and been granted two extensions of time to file the statement and at no time having decided that appellant's claim was without merit, the Local

---

5. 523 F.2d 306 (1975).

allowed the final deadline to pass without filing the statement or requesting a further extension. At this point the Local did not inform either appellant or GM that it had decided to continue or to stop processing appellant's grievance. Such negligent handling of the grievance, unrelated as it was to the merits of appellant's case, amounts to arbitrary representation. It is a clear example of arbitrary and perfunctory handling of a grievance.[6]

The union argued nevertheless that Ruzicka was barred from pressing his claim before the federal court by reason of his failure to exhaust his internal remedies. The court rejected this argument, stating:

Appellant's diligent processing of his complaint through 27 months of intra-Union proceedings is far more than "at least some opportunity" for Local 166 to resolve its dispute with him. The requirement of exhaustion of intra-Union remedies is bottomed on the hope that such procedures will quickly resolve disputes without the delay inherent in the judicial process and with the aid of persons experienced at resolving member-union conflicts short of a full-blown judicial proceeding. When that hope has failed, however, the member is not barred from proceeding to federal court with a claim of unfair representation. To conclude otherwise would allow a union to prevent any claim against it from reaching the stage of litigation by forcing aggrieved members through endless stages of review.[7]

Judge Wade McCree, the former Public Review Board member, filed a special concurring opinion. He did not touch upon the issue of exhaustion of remedies, but did state that he disagreed that the neglect to file a timely statement of unadjusted grievance constitutes arbitrary or perfunctory conduct, since these are adjectives characterizing intentional conduct, that is capricious or superficial. McCree said, however, that he believed that a total failure to act, whether negligent or intentional, except for a proper reason, is behavior so egregious that, as in the case of bad faith, hostility, discrimination, arbitrariness, or perfunctoriness, the union should be held responsible.

As noted, Ruzicka's claim of improper processing of his grievance never reached either the International Executive Board or the Public Review Board. It is safe to say, however, that the Public Review Board would have rejected his claim, since it had already decided that the committeeman's conduct was not willful and that negligent conduct does not amount to fraud, discrimination, or collusion with management.

Not long ago, the Public Review Board undertook a searching analysis of its jurisdiction in grievance cases, and was invited by counsel for an aggrieved UAW member to expand its notion of what constitutes a breach of the duty of fair representation by stating that arbitrary, perfunctory, or even negligent conduct could constitute a constructive fraud

6. 90 LRRM 2500.
7. 90 LRRM at 2501.

upon a member of the union who has, in effect, contracted with the union to represent him in all manner of relations with his employer. The board rejected this invitation, however, and held that the forms of conduct which the union's membership had described in its constitution involved elements of intentional conduct.[8]

The Ruggirello Case

Ruzicka, while it spelled out a notion of what form of conduct breaches the duty of fair representation, did not reach the question of whether a member might be required to exhaust remedies that are fundamentally more limited in scope than those afforded by the courts. That issue, however, might have been squarely posed as a result of another decision by a judge of the United States District Court for the Eastern District of Michigan in *Ruggirello* v. *Ford Motor Co.*[9] Ruggirello was terminated by Ford Motor Company, as a "10-day quit." He claims he was terminated while on a valid medical leave of absence and that he went immediately to his local to file a grievance. He further claims, however, that his committeeman told him the termination was a mistake and that the union would file appropriate documents to have him reinstated with back-pay. Therefore he did not file a grievance, and the union was never able to effect Ruggirello's reinstatement. Ruggirello sued, claiming a breach of the duty of fair representation and, relying upon *Ruzicka,* the district court concluded that a claim for breach of the duty of fair representation had been asserted. But it also concluded that Ruggirello had failed to exhaust his internal union remedies. The court observed:

In this case, counsel for the union asserts that resort to the union's appeals procedure in fact would not have been futile, because the union does have the capacity to provide the monetary relief that Ruggirello seeks. It is also *possible* that article 33, § 8(b) of the 1972 UAW Constitution would be interpreted in light of this circuit's recent decision in *Ruzicka,* to allow relief for union negligence, such as Ruggirello has alleged.

Since resolution of this dispute by resort to the union's own appeals procedure is possible, and since such resolution of employee grievances is preferable to judicial resolution, the unions are hereby ordered to process as timely Ruggirello's complaint about the handling of his grievance as an internal union appeal. This court will retain and exercise jurisdiction in the event that Ruggirello's claims are not settled by these means.[10]

The court, therefore, denied the union's motion for summary judgment and retained jurisdiction. Unfortunately the issue will not be posed by this case; for reasons unknown, Ruggirello never pursued the remedy

---

8. Badura v. Local Union 93, UAW, PRB Case No. 322 (1976).
9. 411 F. Supp. 758, 92 LRRM 2229 (1976).
10. 92 LRRM 2229 at 2231 (emphasis added).

afforded him by the court and his case was recently dismissed as a consequence.

I do not believe, however, that one needs a crystal ball to predict the ultimate resolution of the unanswered question posed by *Ruzicka* and *Ruggirello*. It is plain that the standard of review of grievance processing appeals applied by the Public Review Board under the constitution of the UAW no longer tracks the standard encompassed by the law developed by the courts in determining duty of fair representation claims. Thus, in those claims in which arbitrariness, perfunctoriness, or negligence is asserted as the basis for alleged breach of the duty, resort to the Public Review Board will likely be regarded as futile. As a result, there will be fewer and fewer cases in which the courts will require UAW members to exhaust their internal remedies before asserting a breach of the duty of fair representation in these forums.

This, of course, need not be the case. The UAW obviously may choose to amend its constitution to assert flatly that a member may contest a claim of the breach of duty of fair representation within the internal remedies system up to and including the Public Review Board. Such an action would, I suggest, require much less boldness than was entailed in establishing the board in the first place; yet in terms of its impact upon the UAW membership, it could be at least as significant. It has been our experience that in any given year at least 33 to 40 percent of the appeals presented to the Public Review Board involve the processing of grievances, and in the twenty years' experience of the board, only once has a member been able to establish that elements of fraud, discrimination, or collusion with management affected the processing of his grievance. In that case the board was called upon to affirm a similar, although unstated, conclusion of the International Executive Board.

On the other hand, the message that public review boards can constitute true effective alternative forums to which the courts will largely defer is written plainly in other areas in which the Public Review Board deals. In areas such as Title I — Bill of Rights for Union Members and Title IV — Election Remedies, the constitution of the UAW provides relief for forms of conduct at least as broad as those provided for by statute. In these areas the courts have been uniformly willing to require exhaustion of internal union remedies and to defer largely to board conclusions. Furthermore, there are but a few cases reported in these areas involving the UAW, since an effective remedy is provided and has the distinct advantage of being free. Lawyers are used infrequently by either side in proceedings before the board, and the board's staff is instructed to assist UAW members in properly formulating their claims within the internal remedies system.

More Boards in the Future?

Given the potential effectiveness of the Public Review Board in forestalling legal claims by members against their unions, it is perhaps surprising that the institution has not been more widely imitated. One barrier might be the cost, but I would suggest that there are less expensive means of accomplishing the same end with smaller boards, regional boards, or even single neutrals. More likely, however, it is the basic conservatism of the labor movement that makes other unions fail to give serious consideration to establishing their own public review boards or systems of impartial review. Certainly the climate that gave impetus to the UAW to establish a public review board is absent today. Unions do understand bottom lines of dollars and cents, however, and if altruistic motivations will not provide the impetus for the establishment of effective neutral tribunals, perhaps the basic costs of litigation with the organizations' own members will. Attorneys have become increasingly ingenious in attacking union conduct, particularly in the area of duty of fair representation, and in recent years some very large judgments have been reported. While an effective impartial review system would also be expected to redress damage caused by breaches of the duty of fair representation, at least unions could avoid having to litigate these issues in the presence of hostile juries, which may regard unions as simply another manifestation of large, powerful, wealthy institutions that can well afford to "recompense" injured members.

One obvious drawback to serving claims of the breach of duty of fair representation before impartial tribunals as opposed to the courts is that jurisdiction can be obtained only over the union, and the scope of relief is thus limited to the recovery of damages. The UAW has met this problem in its most recent round of negotiations with the "big three" auto companies by persuading the companies to agree to reinstate grievances when it is found by an internal union tribunal that a member's right to fair representation has been breached. This bit of ingenuity demonstrates the resiliency of the labor union movement when confronted with serious problems. It is hoped that the UAW, confronted by the realization that its own internal remedies system fails to provide the relief its members can obtain in court, will remedy that situation by addressing the constitutional deficiency.

The Absence of Fair Representation

Thomas R. Donahue

The basic elements affecting the opportunity for fair representation all too often account for the absence of that opportunity. The fact is that for more than 50 million American workers there is no opportunity for any kind of representation — fair or otherwise. A small portion of these workers have made the conscious decision they do not want or need representation — and we wish them well. A large number, particularly employees of many state and local governments, are denied any fair representation by law. They have been made wards of the state, second-class citizens, or "servants," as in "public servants."

The largest number have a spelled-out, legal right to representation, but that right has been systematically denied by employer coercion, outright intimidation, and fear. They are not much better off than the employees of one of the nation's coal operators, who declared in an earlier and only slightly darker day of labor-management relations: "The rights and interests of the laboring man will be protected and cared for, not by labor agitators, but by the Christian gentlemen to whom God in his infinite wisdom has given control of the property interests of this country, and upon the successful Management of which so much depends."[1]

You have heard it said: "[Unions] may have been justified in the long past...I think the workmen were not always treated justly. [But there is] no necessity for labor unions...no benefit or advantage through them will accrue to anyone except the union labor leaders...." The speaker is Elbert Gary, chairman of U.S. Steel, and the year is 1921. The rhetoric is a bit more uptempo now. It is more like this sample from a recent right-to-work committee fund-raising letter: "We may soon see strongarm toughs come into your town [and] force honest workmen from their jobs. [The situs picketing bill would] give added muscle to a few of the most corrupt, ruthless and violent union bosses." Now really, is that to be the level of debate?

One good thing, though, they have abandoned the credo of Jay Gould, whose theory on keeping labor in its place was simple: "Hire

---

1. George F. Baer in his "Divine Right" letter written to a Wilkes Barre photographer in 1902, quoted in Richard B. Morris, ed., *The American Worker*, bicentennial edition (Washington, D.C.: U.S. Department of Labor, 1976), p. 162.

one-half of the working class to kill the other half." And they have replaced "Chowderhead" Cohen, described by one veteran of the sit-down strikes in the rubber industry as "266 pounds of stool-pigeon."

Now, instead you can hire a management representative and a labor lawyer, for $6,000 plus travel expenses, to lead a seminar on "How to Maintain Non-Union Status." They advocate deposition where Cohen used a billy, but the results are the same—the destruction of the human spirit.

Their roots are written in the hearing record of the Senate Civil Liberties Committee, headed by Robert LaFollette. They are in the 2,500 leading corporations who relied on spies, stool pigeons, and agent provocateurs to carry out antiunion activities. They are in the three detective agencies that specialized in "industrial security," employing 3,871 operatives to report on union affairs, stir up trouble and, frustrate union organization. They are in the combine of companies that spent more than $9.4 million for spies, strikebreakers, and ammunition.

"The public cannot afford to let this challenge presented by industrial espionage go unnoticed," the committee declared. "Through it, private corporations dominate their employees, deny them their constitutional rights, promote disorder and disharmony, and even set at naught the powers of the government itself."[2]

That report and the "stars" of it—the Bergoff Industrial Service, Harry Bennett, the Mohawk Valley Formula, the Memorial Day Massacre—were scene setters for the National Labor Relations Act (NLRA), the Wagner Act, labor's Magna Carta.

Less dramatic but equally compelling is the hearing record established just last year by Representative Thompson and his Labor-Management Relations Subcommittee. The fears and frustrations; the hassle; the domination of body, mind, and soul; the worries about family and future—they are the same. What is different is that forty-two years ago there was no law.

What the NLRA gave workers—and what we still seek fulfillment of forty-two years later—is a statement of policy:

It is...the policy of the United States...[to encourage] the practice and procedure of collective bargaining...by protecting the exercise by workers of full freedom of association, self-organization, and designation of representatives of their own choosing, for the purpose of negotiating the terms and conditions of their employment or other mutual aid or protection.[3]

It is easy to forget, given the preoccupation of historians and the materialism of today's society, that the early struggles of workers were not

---

2. Report of the La Follette Civil Liberties Committee quoted in Adrian A. Paradis, *The Labor Reference Book* (Philadelphia: Chilton Book Co., 1972), p. 99.
3. 29 U.S.C.A. 151 at 151.

only for better wages, improved working conditions, and job security. They were struggles for representation, for a right to a voice of their own, and for human dignity.

Perhaps the Supreme Court said it best in passing on the constitutionality of the Wagner Act:

Employees have as clear a right to organize and select their representatives for lawful purposes as [a company] has to organize its business and select its own officers and agents. Discrimination and coercion to prevent the free exercise of the right of employees to self-organization and representation is a proper subject for condemnation by competent legislative authority. Long ago we stated the reason for labor organizations. We said that they were organized out of necessities of the situation, that a single employee was helpless in dealing with an employer ... that union was essential [for workers] to deal on an equality with their employer. ... [4]

Unions arose out of the same conditions that gave birth to the nation —the need and demand for representation. Yet, the right to organize and bargain collectively—the law of the land for some forty-two years and as fundamental to democracy as the Bill of Rights—is as far away today for millions of workers as it was before the Wagner Act. Those who place property rights ahead of human rights continue to oppose their employees' attempts to exercise their right to representation through all legal, illegal, or extralegal methods at their command.

As businessmen, those employers cannot be blind to the positive impacts of collective bargaining and of unions in terms of increased living standards, improved working conditions, and increased consumer buying power. Collective bargaining has transformed the industrial scene from a chaotic jungle where robber barons and petty freebooters operated without regard for the needs and rights of human beings into an orderly situation in which mutual problems can be considered and dealt with in a rational manner. It has contributed immeasurably to industrial stability by providing a mechanism for the discussion, hammering out, and resolution of labor-management problems. In economic, social, and human terms, collective bargaining has worked—not perfectly, but it has worked.

In fact, industrial democracy must be the greatest fear of today's junior grade Jay Goulds. After all, the essence of democracy is that people count more than money, and when these corporations can no longer buy the political, economic, and coercive power that gives them domination, then what are they left with? It is no surprise, then, that a war chest of more than $2 million is being raised to fight labor law reforms—to fight the effort to make whole those workers' rights guaranteed in the NLRA.

---

4. NLRB v. Jones & Laughlin Steel Corp., 301 U.S. 1 (1937) at 33, 57 S. Ct. 615 at 622.

After all, it was the National Association of Manufacturers (NAM) that demanded — in 1903 — in a Declaration of Principle: "No person shall be refused employment or in any way discriminated against on account of membership or non-membership in any labor organization."[5]

The so-called principle of the open shop—a "principle" still enforced today by blacklists and mass firings of union sympathizers — is a goal of business, which they "sell" to states under the guise of "right-to-work" laws. "Right-to-freeload" laws, which exist in twenty states in nearly identical terms to the 1903 declaration of the NAM and purport to offer rights to workers, actually operate to deprive workers of their right to self-organization. Where is the "right," if the sole purpose and intent are to frustrate and deprive workers of their rights under the nation's labor law?

The NLRA was based on the innocent belief that most employers would respect the clearly stated rights of their employees. Thus, it granted the National Labor Relations Board (NLRB) only the most limited enforcement powers.

In fact, in a speech to the 1935 AFL convention, J. Warren Madden, first chairman of the NLRB, justified the "reasonable and moderate" remedies and the lack of self-enforcement powers on the basis of protecting the "due process" rights of employers. After all, he suggested, once they know good from evil, "Christian gentlemen" will follow the path of righteousness.

When employers got their chance to rewrite the law in 1947 and 1959, they sought — and obtained — prompt, effective, harsh, even vindictive penalties against union violations. Scripture for the employers; the whip and the chair for unions. The new law established that violations of equal severity, of equal damage to the precepts of the law, are to be treated with unequal punishment. It is not unlike the criminal justice system, where a blue-collar worker goes to jail over a barroom scuffle, while a company that bribes or makes massive illegal political contributions or indeed kills with kepone or vinyl chloride gets off with, at worst, a fine.

There is something seriously wrong with the way the nation's labor law is being enforced and with the strength of its protections. Well, we think we know what is wrong. We think it is time to make the NLRA work again and to restore balance to the nation's labor law. Here are our suggestions for doing just that.

First, we want elections, where no major legal issue is involved, within a specified limited period. We want prompt procedures for unit determinations and representation questions.

5. *The Preliminary Convention of the Citizens' Industrial Association of America* (Chicago: 1903), p. 3.

Delay is the number one tactic of those who seek to prevent workers from exercising their rights — the name of the game is to prevent the election and chill the union off. Consider what Senator Humphrey's or Mr. Ford's reaction would have been if their elections could have been delayed for several months.

Second, we want prompt enforceable decisions in cases concerning whether workers have chosen a union to represent them and whether their employer is required by law to bargain with that union. At present, interminable delays both in ballot counting and in issuing orders to bargain are depriving workers of their right to collective bargaining. If workers succeed in getting — and winning — an NLRB election, the complex of procedures established to guarantee employers "due process" work to deny workers their rights and the justice that is theirs by law and by right.

An employer can stall bargaining for a couple of years, risking no more than an order to begin bargaining, which the Board cannot enforce. Once that order comes, the employer can just sit at the table and refuse to bargain in good faith. His penalty, which can take as long as two years to be handed down, is an unenforceable cease-and-desist order. Even then, the employer has one more option: "surface bargaining" or holding out for impossible terms.

The workers have three options: (1) accept the degrading offer; (2) give up and disband the union; (3) go out on strike and face replacement and permanent loss of their jobs. This situation is not much different from the homestead worker who in 1894 responded to Hamlin Garland's question on how he stood on the strike: "It's all foolishness," the worker replied, "men working for less than two dollars can't afford to strike." In other words, for many workers today, the price of their rights is economic ruin for themselves and their families. When the price of freedom is so high, freedom becomes expendable for a little security.

Third, we want preliminary injunctions to prevent employers from discriminatory discharges of workers for exercising their right to organize and for illegal refusals to bargain after elections. Firing has always been a favorite employer tactic. It is so final, so definitive — it really lets a man know where he stands: outside the plant for a couple years before the Board remedies the wrong.

Fourth, we want to reduce the time required for a final decision in unfair labor practice cases. While we seek no changes in the law governing what is an unfair labor practice, we recognize that the Board is administratively unable to handle its present caseload, which has doubled as a result of the 1947 and 1959 amendments. We believe along with the American Bar Association that the Board should be expanded to nine members and given authority to streamline its procedures. We seek to deny no party their day in court; we just want to ensure that day and hasten it.

Fifth, we want the Board to have authority to issue self-enforcing orders. This would deprive no one of his right to appeal; rather it would enhance the authority of the Board and reduce the number of frivolous appeals.

Sixth, we want the Congress to clarify certain definitional provisions — such as "successorship" — which have resulted in erroneous or contradictory decisions.

Seventh, we want the government to stop subsidizing employers who consistently and repeatedly violate the law. Government contracts are not awarded to companies that violate laws against race or sex discrimination or ignore pollution controls. The same must apply for the nation's labor law or the government will be promoting the breaking of laws it is supposed to enforce—an interesting moral, as well as legal, proposition.

Eighth, we want Section 14(b) repealed. This section, which permits states to weaken the national standards the federal government has established for labor law, is contrary to the concept of a truly uniform national labor law.

There is nothing un-American about the union shop. It is an American institution—a microcosm of the entire political system under which all may vote and the majority rules. All must abide by the rule of the majority, always with the opportunity for the minority to become the majority.

The national labor law states on the one hand that unions are obligated to provide fair representation to every worker covered by the collective bargaining agreement. In twenty states, on the other hand, the law says that no worker is obligated to pay his portion of the cost of that fair representation. In fact, the union cannot even seek such a provision.

Permit me an analogy: In many farm states—and farm states have a particular propensity to be "right-to-work" states — commodity commissions have been established to conduct research on and to promote certain crops, such as peas or lentils. Every farmer is assessed so much per hundredweight to support the activities of the commission, because they all benefit from the research and promotion.

It seems to me that if a union shop is "compulsory unionism," then commodity commissions are "compulsory commissionism." Yet there are some differences, of course. A union must be voted in by a majority of the workers; it only takes a majority of the legislature to vote in a commodity commission. Union officers are elected by secret ballot election; commodity commission members are generally appointed by a governor. Union members generally get to vote on their proposed contract; farmers do not get to vote on what a commission is going to do. Unions must have the employer's approval and agreement before a union-shop clause can be written in a contract; commodity commissions are empowered by the state to assess every farmer. One more difference is that unions represent people; commodity commissions represent products.

The NAM had one thing in mind when it proposed the open-shop language that has been bought by twenty states under the guise of giving workers a "right": the right to work for less; the right to weaken strong unions; the right to destroy weak unions. The NAM did not want to obligate unions to provide better, fairer representation; they do not want representation, period.

There is a two-edged sword here. On one side, cut into union finances by forcing unreasonable demands on them to provide fair representation to nonmembers; on the other side, slice into union strength by denying them financial assistance from all workers. The question is not more power for the union bosses or a return of Jay Gould. It is a question of human rights, most profoundly stated by a black man on the picket line in Memphis in 1968. His sign read: "I am a Man." If America is to stand for human rights in Russia and Chile, it must stand for human rights in Roanoke Rapids and Charlotte.

There are many phrases for what we seek—equal protection, justice, balance, fairness, law-and-order, equity—but the basic proposition is that if law is to mean something in America, then the law must be applied equally and across-the-board with equal fairness, equal justice, equal sanction. Before the law, labor and management must stand equal. Every worker—in public as well as private employment—must have the right to self-organization and collective bargaining, with speedy processes and effective remedies to protect those rights.

Contributors

Benjamin Aaron, professor of law, University of California at Los Angeles; chairman of the U.S. Branch of the International Society for Labor Law and Social Security and member of the Society's International Executive Board; past service with the National War Labor Board, National Wage Stabilization Board, and numerous government and presidential fact-finding, emergency, and arbitration boards; formerly director of the UCLA Institute of Industrial Relations, president of the National Academy of Arbitrators and the Industrial Relations Research Association, and secretary of the Section of Labor Relations Law, American Bar Association; author and editor of numerous books and articles on industrial relations and labor law in both the private and the public sectors.

Thomas R. Donahue, executive assistant to AFL-CIO President George Meany; formerly executive secretary, Service Employees' International Union; assistant secretary of labor, U.S. Department of Labor.

James E. Jones, Jr., professor of law and industrial relations, University of Wisconsin; member, Wisconsin Manpower Planning Council, National Advisory Board of the Industrial Relations Law Journal, and National Advisory Committee of the National Bar Association's Equal Employment Clinical Project; President, Madison Police and Fire Commission; formerly director, Office of Labor Management Policy Development and associate solicitor of labor, Division of Labor Relations and Civil Rights, U.S. Department of Labor; author of books and articles on national emergency disputes and employment discrimination.

David Y. Klein, counsel, Public Review Board, United Automobile, Aerospace, and Agricultural Implement Workers of America; attorney for several unions ranging from the building trades to the American Association of University Professors; author of numerous scholarly articles on public review boards.

Richard Lipsitz, attorney and member of Lipsitz, Green, Fahringer, Roll, Schuller and James law firm, Buffalo, New York, which has represented a large variety of labor organizations since 1949; visiting lecturer at New York State School of Industrial and Labor Relations, 1974–75; arbitrator, outside New York State; member, Executive Committee of the New York State Bar Association, Labor Law Section, and counsel for the New York Civil Liberties Union, Niagara Frontier Chapter.

Jean T. McKelvey, professor emeritus, New York State School of Industrial and Labor Relations; visiting professor, Cornell Law School; member, Public Review Board, United Automobile, Aerospace, and Agricultural Implement Workers of America; member, Federal Service Impasses Panel; past president, National Academy of Arbitrators.

Robert J. Rabin, professor of law, Syracuse University Law School; formerly attorney for Amalgamated Clothing Workers of America and National Education Association; author of various articles on arbitration and the duty of fair representation.

Clyde W. Summers, Fordham Professor of Law, University of Pennsylvania School of Law; member, International Society of Labor Law and Social Legislation, and National Academy of Arbitrators; formerly Garver Professor of Law, Yale University School of Law; author of numerous articles published in law reviews, other periodicals, conference reports, and symposia; primary areas of scholarly interest include: internal union problems and rights of individual workers and constitutional rights and civil liberties.

Judith P. Vladeck, attorney and member of Vladeck, Elias, Vladeck and Lewis law firm, New York City; represents union clients in all aspects of labor-management matters, including negotiations, arbitration, appearance before administrative agencies, and litigation; part-time extension faculty member, New York State School of Industrial and Labor Relations.